Motifs for
Crazy Quilting

J. Marsha Michler

Published by

krause publications
An F&W Publications Company

700 East State Street • Iola, WI 54990-0001
715-445-2214 • 888-457-2873
www.krause.com

Please call or write for our free catalog of publications. To place an order or obtain a free catalog, please call (800) 258-0929.
Photography by J. Marsha Michler (unless otherwise stated)
Illustrations by J. Marsha Michler

Library of Congress Catalog Number 2002107606
ISBN 0-87349-427-X

Motifs for Crazy Quilting

Special thanks to Sandy Taylor my agent, Christine Townsend, my editor, Marilyn McGrane, cover artist and book designer. Thanks to my suppliers for the wonderful things to play with: Dena Lenham of Kreinik Manufacturing. Co. Inc., Vickie Smith of YLI, Maggie Backman of Things Japanese, Vikkie Clayton with her exquisite hand-dyes, Lois Caron of The Caron Collection. Thanks to Pokey of *Quilting Arts* magazine for running the article on the dragon shawl. My gratitude to Dee Stark for her expertise, and to Rod Byam for the use of the photos, and to Steven for doing the painting which appears on page 6. Many thanks to Cindy and Geri of the Limerick Public Library for friendly and helpful research assistance.

Credit is due to Laura Barr Lougee's book, *The Web of the Spider*, 1964, which helped me to better understand spider webs, and Mary Alice Sullivan's book, *Woman's World: A Complete Guide to Perfect Womanhood*, 1894, for Victorian flower meanings. Many other resources are too numerous to mention. At the same time, and on the same note, I'd like to refer my readers to their local libraries for more pictorial ideas than what can be contained on these 144 pages – may your search be enjoyable and prolific!

Suppliers of the threads and other materials featured in this book include:

Silk Mori®, Silk Serica®, Japan Gold and Silver, Metallics:
Kreinik Manufacturing. Co., Inc.
3106 Timanus Ln., Ste. 101
Baltimore, MD 21244
(800) 537-2166
http://www.kreinik.com

Silk Ribbon, Basting Thread:
YLI Corporation
161 W. Main St.
Rock Hill, SC 29730
(800) 296-8139
www.ylicorp.com

Waterlilies®, Soie Crystale®, Impressions®:
The Caron Collection Ltd.
55 Old South Ave.
Stratford, CT 06615
(203) 381-9999
www.caron-net.com

Silk Perle in sizes #8 and #12, Silk Chenille (hand-dyed):
Victoria Clayton
6448 Freeman Rd.
Byron, NY 14422-9720
(716) 548-2620
http://www.hand-dyedfibers.com

Buttonhole silk, Silk dyes:
Things Japanese
9805 N.E. 116th Ste. 7160
Kirkland, WA 98034-4248
www.silkthings.com

Empress Silk Threads®
Needle Necessities, Inc.
7211 Garden Grove Blvd. Ste. B&C
Garden Grove, CA 92841
(714) 892-9211
www.needlenecessities.com

Paternayan® Persian Wool Threads
JCA, Inc.
35 Scales Ln.
Townsend, MA 01469
(978) 597-8794

Glass Seed Beads
Shipwreck Beads
2500 Mottman Rd. SW
Olympia, WA 98512
(360) 754-2323
www.shipwreck-beads.com

Table of Contents

The Tracing Paper Transfer
Technique 141

Steps in Making a Crazy Quilt 142

Other Works by this Author 144

Index 144

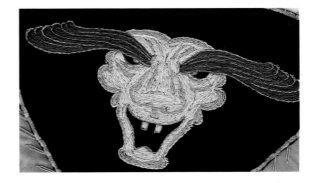

Introduction

Essential to the most beautiful of crazy quilts are the handworked motifs and patternings on the interiors of the patches. These bring art to the crazy quilt, enlivening its surface with creative imagery. This book is intended to give you ideas for motifs, and to demonstrate some of the creative ways they can be replicated.

The possibilities for creating motifs are endless. This book contains a sampling of ideas in the form of full-size diagrams, and some ways to create original motifs of your own. There are many ways to replicate a plain, line-drawn design and turn it into something spectacular. These include using embroidery stitches, and other, dimensional methods such as ribbonwork and beading. Mixing media creates dimension and texture, making a design more interesting.

The designs can be used in the same size as they are given, or enlarged or reduced on a photocopier. Enlarge a motif, for instance, to use it as a quilt center. Make a motif smaller to fit into a small area. Replicate a motif to be used as a repeated border design.

This book is designed for use with my previous three books on crazy quilting (you'll find them listed at the end of the book). They include methods of making crazy quilts and other projects, embroidery stitches, embellishment techniques with how-to's, and finishing methods.

Not for embroidery alone, the designs in this book are adaptable to other forms of creativity, as well. Here, Steven painted an adaptation of the morning glory motif (page 77) on a board that will become a rack with shaker pegs on it.

General Information

Collecting Threads

Collect as many different types of hand-embroidery threads as you can; there will be a use for just about anything you can find. Flosses are used to work solid fillers in motifs using stitches such as satin stitch and long and short stitch. Flosses from different manufacturers are unique in their characteristics, especially in the silks. The thickness of the thread, its twist, and sheen create variations from one brand to another.

Twisted threads such as Buttonhole silks, Soie Perlee, and Silk Perle add dimension and texture, and are wonderful

Threads for fill-in embroidery consist of mainly multi-stranded flosses. These separate into individual strands, and can be used single strand, double, triple or more strands in the needle. Shown here are the silks: Kreinik's Mori, The Caron Collection's Soie Crystale and Waterlilies, Soie D'Alger, and Empress.

Threads for working lines of embroidery along the edges of patches are single-strand twisted threads as well as exotic and other fibers that can be sewn through the fabric or couched to its surface. Shown are the silks: Soie Perlee, Kreinik's Serica and Bella, Buttonhole silk, Vikki Clayton's hand-dyed Silk Perle threads and silk chenille.

Working with Silk Threads

Most of the illustrated embroidered motifs are worked in silk threads. Silks, at first, may seem a little fussy to work with, but their beautiful colors and luster make them well worth the effort. Here are some techniques for handling silks:

- Begin by using a non-greasy hand lotion, and removing any snags from your hands.
- "Strip" the silks when using silk flosses. Cut a working length of the floss then pull out the number of strands needed. Lay them back together to use them. This preparation allows the maximum sheen and other qualities of the thread to show up well.
- If using only one strand, keep it from slipping out of the needle by taking a stitch though the thread near to the eye of the needle. Settle this stitch into the eye of the needle. (This will work with some threads, but not all).
- Use a "laying tool" if needed. A laying tool is no more than a large, blunt needle. As the thread is taken through the fabric to the back, run it over the needle. This prevents twists and snags, and allows the thread to lie flat and show its maximum luster. You will need to have the work in a lap hoop in order to have both hands free to stitch.

for outlining motifs in addition to working embroidery along patch seams.

Threads too thick to sew through fabric can be couched. Couching can be used to outline, or fill in motifs.

Cotton threads are the easiest to work with, and are excellent for beginners. Metallic threads add shimmer to a design. Use rayons for their high sheen. Silks are ideal for rendering fine details, and their luster is incomparable ... silks are my preference by far. Most of the embroideries herein were worked in silk threads.

Threads can be located in needlearts shops, catalogs, and by doing a search on the Internet.

Once you find a thread you like, collect it in all (or most) colors. It's hard to have *too* many hues or shades! Think of the colors you use most, and keep a good stash of them; that way you will have what you need when you need it. I always find myself running out of browns, other neutral shades, and greens way before any other colors, so I keep plenty of those on hand.

Below: The edges of patches are embroidered in Silk Serica, Buttonhole Silk, and couched hand-dyed silk chenille.

Top: Patch edges are treated to Vikki Clayton's hand-dyed Silk Perle threads.

Left: Silk ribbons in addition to twisted threads are attractive patch edge treatments.

Bottom: Threads and materials for special purposes include silk ribbons for silk ribbon embroidery, wools for wool embroidery, metallic threads, and seed beads. Shown are YLI's silk ribbons in 4mm and 7mm widths, Paternayan Persian wools, Kreinik's metallics, and seed beads.

Fabrics for Embroidery Backgrounds

The easiest fabrics to embroider are those made of the natural fibers: Cotton, wool, linen, silk, and rayon (rayon is actually a synthetic/natural fiber). Collect a variety of surface textures such as plain weaves, twill, damask, and others. These fabrics can be found in dressmaking and drapery selections. Choose drapery types that are not too heavy, and ones that are un-backed, such as cotton damask or sateen. All of these make beautiful fabrics for crazy patches.

If your finished quilt or project is to be washable, it is necessary to pre-wash all of the fabrics that go into it. It is also a good idea to wash any trims and laces. If threads are not labeled "colorfast," test them by dampening and laying them on a paper towel to see if the dye bleeds. Do not use anything that continually bleeds dye. Because machine washing doesn't allow you to see if dye is running, it is best to wash fabrics by hand. Use a temperature appropriate for the fabric and a mild soap. Rinse well, line dry, and press. Any washable, finished article should be washed using the gentlest method possible.

Most natural fabrics are washable, but some may have special finishes that will not survive washing. In this case, a finished quilt may be dry cleaned by a knowledgeable cleaner. It is actually preferable not to clean a quilt at all except by a light vacuuming of its surface. But all depends on how the quilt is used: If it is in active use, such as on a bed, choose washable fabrics to begin with so it can be washed when need be. If it is not handled, such as a wall hanging or a decorative throw, then avoid cleaning except for an occasional light vacuuming. Since an ounce of prevention is worth a pound of cure, though, be sure to start out with a clean quilt: have clean hands while working on your quilt. If you store it, use careful storage methods.

Ideas for Motifs

Learning to draw is perhaps the most useful skill you can acquire. The Oriental motifs on the Dragon Shawl are my own adaptations of designs found on dishes and vases, derived by drawing and redrawing several times to get the feel of the design. Finally, I do my own version, sometimes making adaptations to specifically fit onto a crazy patch.

Possible subject matter is endless. Look around you for ideas. Sketch your home and embroider it. Look to various hobbies and interests. If you like Victorian things, find a reference on Victorian inventions and sketch some of them. A feather fallen onto grass ... a hummingbird in the heart-shaped leaves of the lilac bush: such inspirations are all around!

Adapt the designs found on dishes and other objects.

Theme Quilts

Although a crazy quilt can consist of a variety of images that do not relate to each other, a quilt can also be based on a theme. In a theme quilt, most (or all) of the decor is related to the theme. A theme gives a quilt purpose, and often personalizes it.

Here are some ideas for theme quilts based on the motifs in this book:

A Victorian Language of Flowers quilt

A rebus quilt

An alphabet quilt

A Victoriana quilt (with Victorian objects)

An Oriental quilt

Right: This shawl has an Oriental theme.

Below: This is a quilt with a message (see Rebus on pages 105 to 106), and a Victorian theme.

Embroidery tools include a needle holder (pincushion), scissors, needles, hoops, and a means of thread storage. Check with a needlework supply shop for systems of storing threads. Simply winding opened skeins onto small cards keeps the threads handy and the colors visible. Tucking them into small plastic bags also works well. Be sure to keep track of color names and numbers in case you wish to reorder.

Instructions for Embroidering Motifs

Tools and Materials

> Set of embroidery needles in assorted sizes
> Set of chenille needles in assorted sizes, but especially size 18
> Embroidery scissors or thread clippers
> Embroidery hoop in the style and size of your choice
> Quilter's lap-style hoop for hands-free embroidering
> For transferring designs: tracing paper, pencil, basting thread
> See the individual methods for additional materials

Lighting is important for doing fine embroidery work. I work by daylight as much as possible. When a light becomes necessary, I use a task light fitted with a 25-watt fluorescent bulb, which is roughly comparable with a 100-watt incandescent light. You may like to use a color-corrected bulb, but I find that choosing colors in daylight, then embroidering under fluorescent lighting causes no confusion. Either a task light or an adjustable floor lamp can be moved about and positioned how and where you most need it.

Working the Motifs

Read instructions for each of the methods before beginning a quilt. Some must be worked before the quilt is patched, although most can be worked on a patched quilt top. That is, a patched top that is not yet fastened to a backing.

If you are new to embroidery, the simplest way to embroider any of the designs is outline embroidery (see page 99). If you like, take the next step and fill in parts of the design using any filler stitch (see Fill-in Embroidery on pages 64 to 65).

Make your own creative decisions regarding stitches, colors, and techniques for working the embroideries. Some of the motifs shown are worked in several types of needlework, such

The motif is outlined, and the wheat is worked in silk floss and 4mm silk ribbon. The purple flowers are worked in French knots.

as embroidery stitches added to an applique, or silk ribbon added to thread embroidery.

If you like to stay with the realistic colors of an object, then find a resource showing those. Otherwise, do as I do and fill in with the colors of your choice, creating fantasy objects.

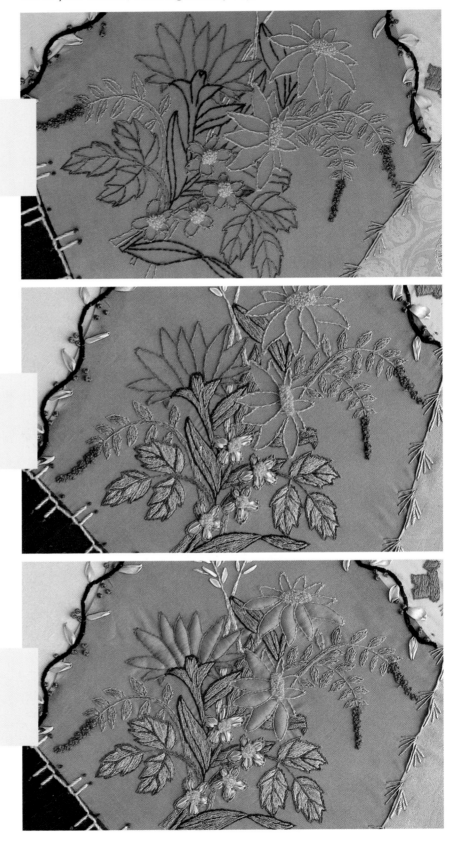

Flower centers are worked in punch needle, in Silk Mori.

Leaves and stems are worked in outline stitch, in Waterlilies. Blue flowers are filled in with 4mm silk ribbon.

Trapunto finishes the flower petals.

Choosing Colors

Choose colors with the intent to either make an embroidery stand out from its background, or blend into its surroundings.

Choose bright, vigorous colors to make an embroidery stand out. Use colors that contrast with the background fabric. Techniques that are dimensional will magnify this effect.

To achieve an antique appearance, use soft, faded colors; they give a faded, old-fashioned look that will appear as if the embroidery was worked many years ago. Since colors fade differently over time, select some colors that are a little brighter than others. And, choose some in off-tones, such as grays instead of greens for leaves, to make it appear as if the true color faded away.

This motif, worked mainly in Silk Mori, looks as if it had just been embroidered.

This motif, worked in muted shades of Waterlilies, appears as if it had been done a hundred or so years ago.

Most of the embroidery stitches for pictorial work are different than those used for the stitches along the patch seams of a crazy quilt. These are either for outlining, or filling in a design. Refer to *The Magic of Crazy Quilting* for stitches to use along patch seams.

Many types of embroidery and embellishments create a "flat" surface, while others are dimensional. Flat techniques include fill-in embroidery, appliqué, couching, shadow work, and others. Dimensional methods include ribbonwork, folded fabric flowers, beading, and wool embroidery. Working a range of techniques on a quilt top creates an interesting play of texture on its surface.

Working Freehand

After the bow (see page 36) was embroidered, silk ribbon embroidered flowers and leaves were added freehand. Florals are especially easy to embroider without following lines. Try embroidering a stem, add some leaves to it, and add one or more flowers. Add more stems, leaves, and flowers and you will soon have a bouquet. The bow and stems were worked in Soie D'Alger.

Building Up Motifs

Many of the diagrammed motifs will benefit from some added details. You can build up more elaborate pictorials by combining motifs. Begin with a horse, for instance, then some land forms (see Landscapes and Scenery, pages 87 to 89); add some clouds, a tree, and so on. Resize the motifs as needed.

A tree and mountains were fitted into an irregular patch. The motif was worked in Waterlilies, with patch edges embroidered in hand-dyed Silk Perles.

Placement of Motifs

Generally, motifs are placed at the centers of patches, but can also be placed into corners and other areas. It is not necessary that a motif fit onto one patch. A motif can be spread over two or more patches on a patched quilt top. Using the Tracing Paper Transfer Technique (page 141), you can easily find the best placement for a motif by moving it around until it seems to "fit."

A tree worked in silk ribbon is spread across four patches.

Planning a Quilt

Getting the motifs to fit within the patches requires a combination of preplanning and pre-embroidering.

Some of the methods in this book require that motifs be made separately from the quilt. Do those motifs first, then patch the quilt. Use the pre-made patches while patching the quilt, and make the quilt's other patches large enough to accommodate additional motifs.

The steps in making a crazy quilt appear on page 142 to 143.

Work embroideries and collect them to make a crazy quilt.

BELGIUM

Motifs and Methods

Enlarge or reduce the designs as needed to fit within the patches. Trace a design, then use a photocopier to enlarge or reduce it. Or, redraw the motif to the size desired.

Combine motifs in various ways to make larger and more elaborate designs. Add a butterfly to a floral, or combine hills, clouds, and trees.

The "Victorian Language of Flowers" is given where meanings could be found (see the section on Flowers, pages 67 to 81). Flower language tends to vary from one Victorian source to another. The one used in this book is from my original 1894 copy of *Woman's World: A Complete Guide to Perfect Womanhood*, by Mary Alice Sullivan, published by Monarch Book Co., Philadelphia, Pennsylvania. More meanings are given in *The Magic of Crazy Quilting*.

Alphabets & Letters

Use alphabets and letters for:

- ❀ Monogramming your quilt with your initials
- ❀ Lettering your name on a quilt
- ❀ Adding the dates during which the quilt was made, or the date the quilt was finished
- ❀ An "ABC" quilt
- ❀ A floral quilt with "A is for Aster," "B is for Begonia," etc.
- ❀ Any type of lettering or wording on a quilt

Alyssum

You may like to embroider the Victorian meaning along with the flower. Hand letter the words, then transfer using the Tracing Paper Transfer Technique (see page 141).

worth beyond beauty

Creating Letters and Adding Lettering to a Crazy Quilt

Using your own handwriting is the simplest way to design lettering. Simply write a letter on a sheet of paper in printing or cursive, making it the size needed. If desired, add flourishes, and/or sketch a floral in and around it.

When the drawing is complete, transfer it to the crazy-pieced quilt top using the Tracing Paper Transfer Technique (see page 141). Embroider along the outlines of the design using outline stitch, backstitch, couching, or any stitch that makes a neat outline.

Fill in the design or parts of it as desired. Block letters can be filled in with any filler stitch of your choice such as satin, chain, long and short, or outline. Work flower stems in outline stitch, and leaves in any stitch that makes a leaf-like shape such as lazy daisy. Flowers as well as leaves can be outlined and filled in, or suggested by silk ribbon stitches.

Always heat-set ink, by placing an iron onto it for about 30 seconds. Use the highest setting suitable for the type of fabric you are working with.

The ink may run a little on some fabrics. Here, bias silk ribbons were used. Tape the fabric or ribbons onto cardboard, do the lettering, and then remove the tape carefully. The raw edges will be pressed under when sewn to the quilt.

Enlarge a letter, then fill it in with the fancy work of your choice. This will make an attractive patch on a crazy quilt.

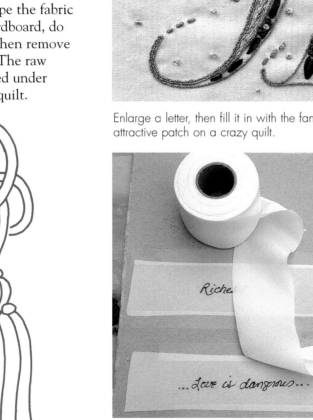

Lettering is easily done using permanent fabric pens. Observe any instructions that came with the pen. Bias-cut silk ribbon is taped to cardboard to make it easier to write on.

A message on a ribbon is added to a bird embroidery. The bird was outlined, then filled in using three shades of Waterlilies.

Block letters are easy to create. Draw two letters, one overlapped onto the other, then connect the lines as shown here. You may like to use a ruler to make your lines nice and even.

Make adaptations of existing lettering:
- Look at the letters used in book and magazine titles, and other printed materials and draw your adaptations of them. Try adding serifs, curved lines, and vary the widths of block letters.
- Using a font on a computer, make the letter the size needed in a layout program, then print it out. Lay a sheet of tracing paper over it, and add your own touches.

Combine letters to form names and monograms. Use your own handwriting, shaping the letters, then arrange them as you like. Add florals, or leave them plain.

Seven Ways to Add Florals to Letters

Intrinsic. The florals take the shape of the letter itself. Embroider in thread or silk ribbon embroidery. Choose stitches that follow the shape of the letter.

Adjacent. Place florals before and after the letter.

Dots and Crossings. Use flowers and vines to dot i's and cross t's.

Entwined. Draw the letter and an interweaving vine, and transfer to fabric. Embroider. Then add flowers and leaves to the vine.

Boxed. Draw a box-shape (or circle, oval, or wreath) around the letter adding florals.

Underlined. Placing a floral beneath a letter has the effect of underlining.

Filler. Use a blossom to fill in the enclosed area(s) of a letter.

Angels

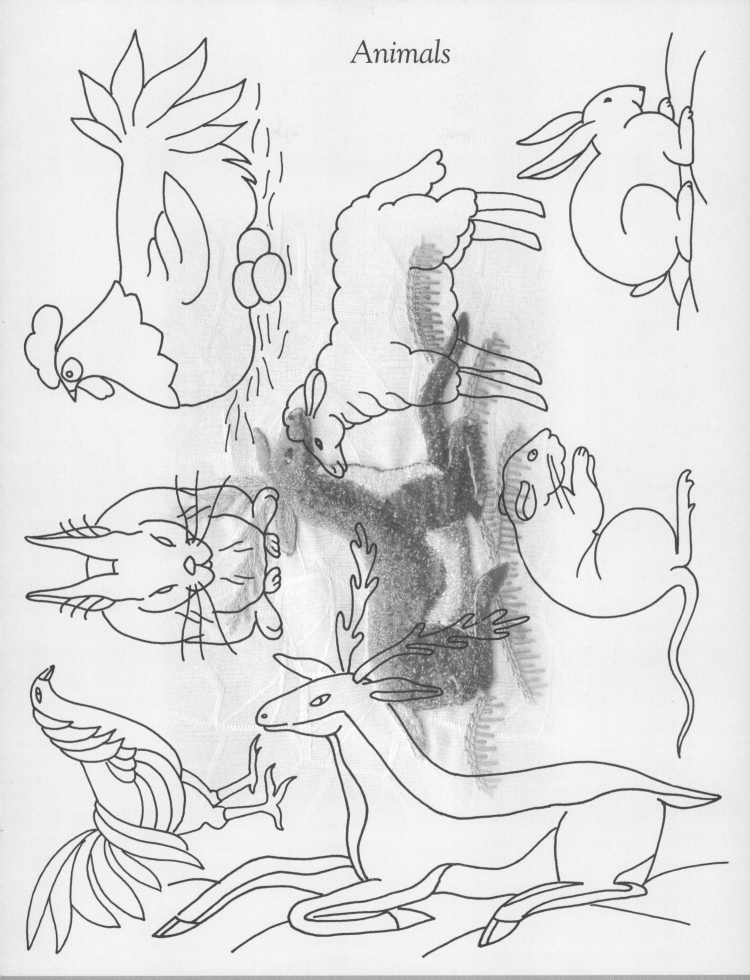

Small scraps of fabric
Size 12 Sharp needle
100 percent cotton or silk
thread to blend with or
match the appliqué fabric,
size 50
Scissors, pins

Appliqué

Appliqués can be worked **before** or **after** the quilt top is patched.

Choose fabrics that hold a crease well, are firmly woven, and resist fraying. 100 percent cottons, rayons, silks, and other natural-fiber fabrics are some of the best choices.

Use simple, basic shapes. Intricate shapes are difficult to work with. Appliqués tend to lose detail as they are stitched.

Appliqués combine beautifully with embroidery and other techniques. Appliqués are ideal for the larger details of a design; fill in the smaller details using embroidery or other methods.

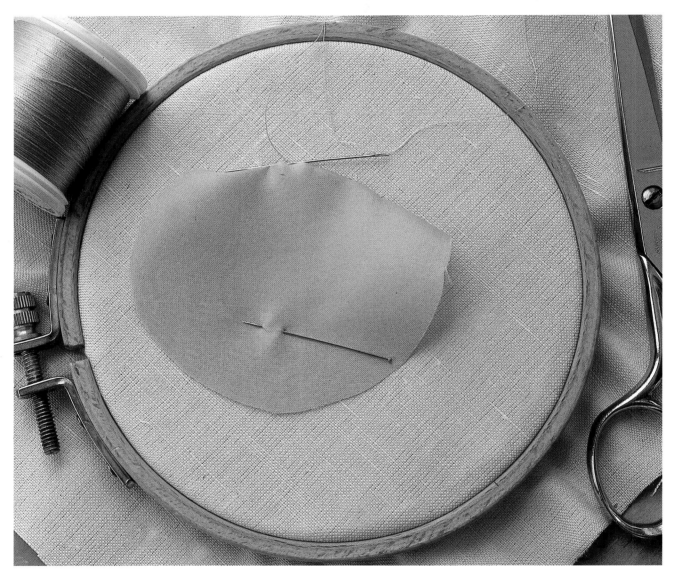

Cut out the fabric in the shape desired adding about 1/8" or a little more for a seam allowance all around. Either press under the seam allowance, or leave it to be folded under as you work. Pin or baste the shape in place onto the background fabric. Thread the needle and secure the end of the thread under the appliqué. Slipstitch invisibly around the appliqué, then fasten off. If you have not pressed the edges under, use the needle to turn the edge under before each stitch (this is called the "needle-turn" method). To make a slipstitch, run the needle inside the fold of the appliqué, pick up a thread or two of the background fabric, and pull through.

Motifs for Appliqué

Teacups are an easy shape to appliqué and make attractive little containers for floral embroideries. Work the handles in embroidery, then work flowery or other designs onto the cups using silk ribbon, threads, or other forms of embroidery. This example was worked in wool threads and fabrics.

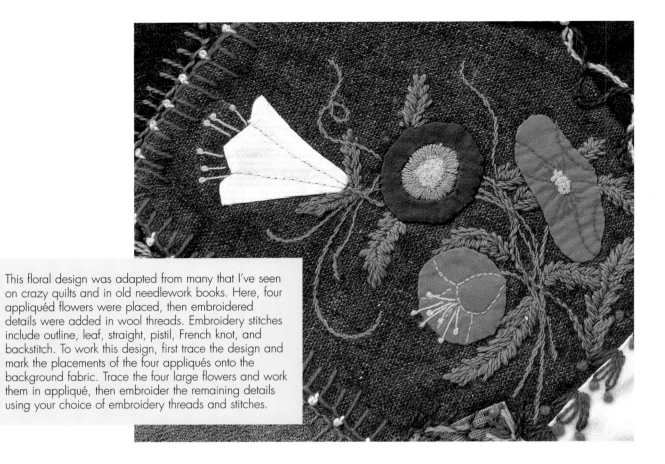

This floral design was adapted from many that I've seen on crazy quilts and in old needlework books. Here, four appliquéd flowers were placed, then embroidered details were added in wool threads. Embroidery stitches include outline, leaf, straight, pistil, French knot, and backstitch. To work this design, first trace the design and mark the placements of the four appliqués onto the background fabric. Trace the four large flowers and work them in appliqué, then embroider the remaining details using your choice of embroidery threads and stitches.

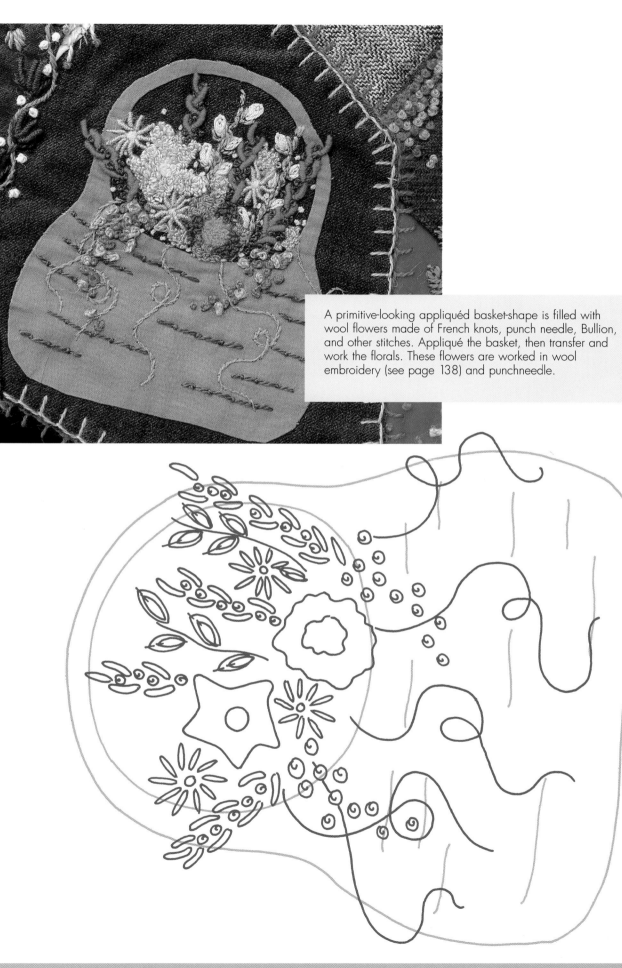

A primitive-looking appliquéd basket-shape is filled with wool flowers made of French knots, punch needle, Bullion, and other stitches. Appliqué the basket, then transfer and work the florals. These flowers are worked in wool embroidery (see page 138) and punchneedle.

Beading

Materials

Size 11 glass seed beads
(other sizes and types of
beads may also be used)
Fine embroidery needle, or a
beading needle and needle
threader
Embroidery hoop
Beading thread

It is best to do beading **last**, after all other embroidery is finished. Be sure to use thread that is made especially for beading. Glass beads can cut through ordinary threads as the beads are being sewn on, or long afterwards. (Quilting or silk threads are not beading thread substitutes.)

Any needle that fits through the bead can be used. Hole sizes among beads can vary in one batch, so find a needle that works for all or most of them. I prefer to use a beading needle because then I'm never hung up by the one bead with a too-small hole. This type of needle is fine and long so you can also string a line of beads onto it if you are doing filler work or outlining. Use a needle threader to thread the needle since beading needles have a very fine eye.

To protect beads that are already sewn on, wrap the embroidery hoop in soft fabric. 100 percent cotton batiste works well. A few stitches will hold the wraps in place. I prefer to use a lap hoop in order to have both hands free for beading. Beading should be done as the final step of embroidering the quilt top. If done earlier, embroidery threads can catch on the beads, making it difficult to embroider.

Sewing on a bead is a simple thing. Simply fasten the thread securely to the back of the fabric and bring the needle up through. Run the needle through the bead, then sew back down again. I like to stitch each bead twice to lock them well into place.

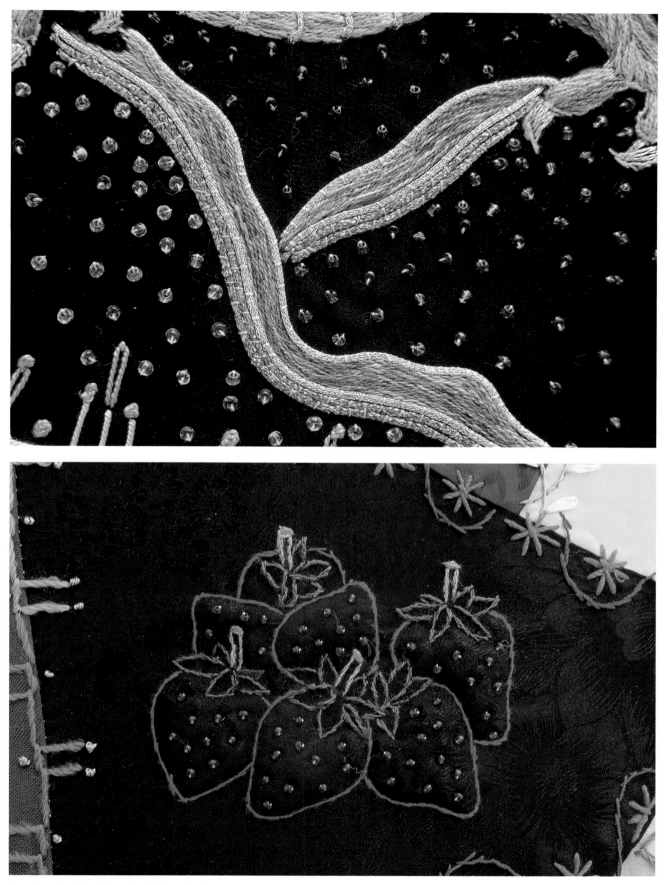

Top: Beads help define the hills under the dragon.

Bottom: Beads enhance the strawberries.

Birds

Motifs for Crazy Quilting

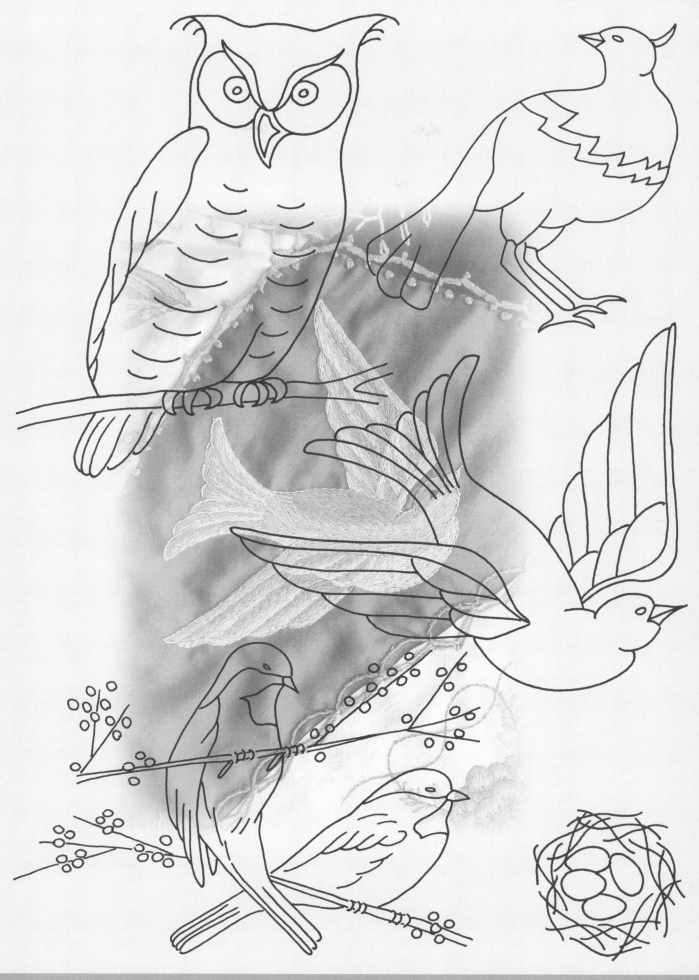

Bows

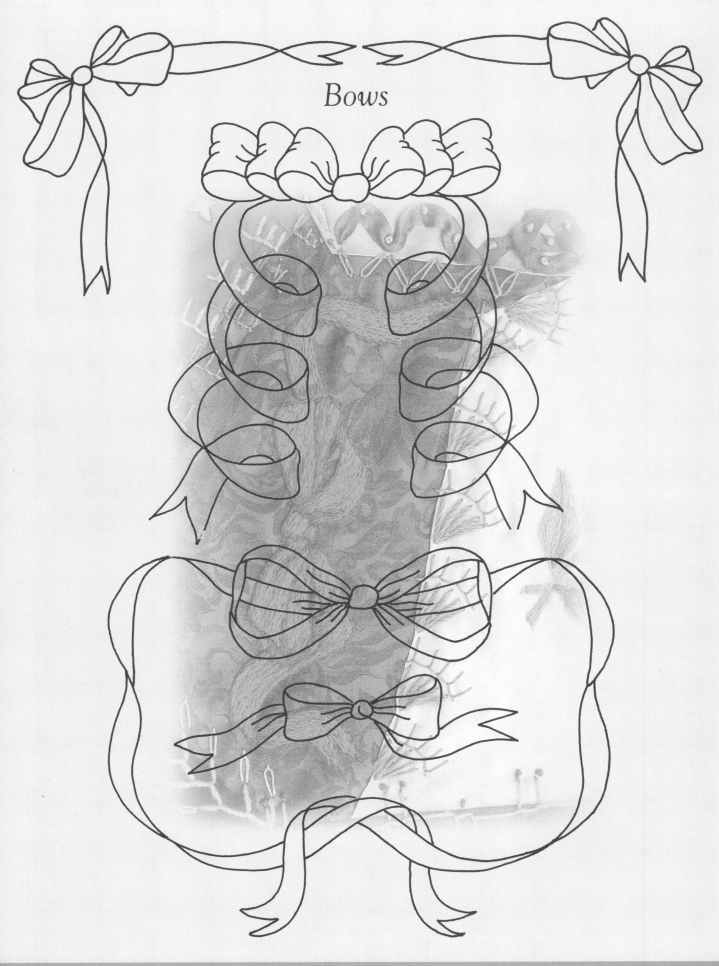

Bric-a-brac

Butterflies
& Bugs

Cats

Clouds

Couching

Materials

Fiber for couching
Sewing thread or embroidery
 thread
Embroidery needle to fit the
 thread
Large needle (such as a size
 18) chenille needle

Couching is best done **after** the quilt top is patched in order to have a place to anchor the thread ends.

Couching consists of fastening a material to the surface of fabric by sewing it on with thread or embroidery floss. Some materials such as narrow ribbons, braids, yarns, metallics, and heavy threads are too thick or too delicate to sew through fabric; to apply them, they must be couched. It is a useful technique for outlining motifs, for filler work, or for adding decoration to an embroidery.

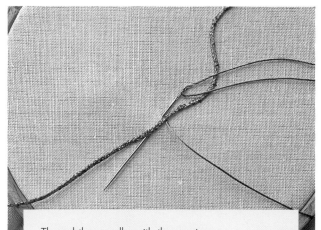

Thread the needle with the sewing or embroidery thread and fasten onto the back of the background fabric. Lay the couching material on the background fabric. Bring the needle up through, and make small stitches over the couching material to hold it in place. Fasten off.

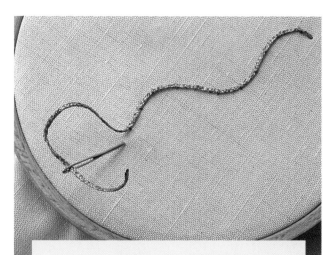

Use a large needle to bring the ends of the couching material to the back.

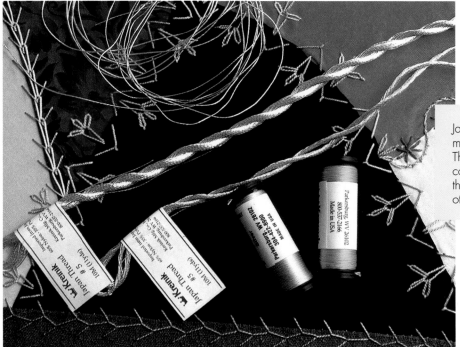

Japan threads consist of tinsel-like metals wound around a fiber core. They are delicate and must be couched. The spools are silk threads for couching japans and other metal threads.

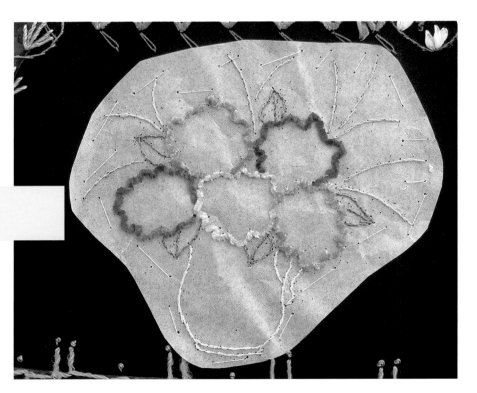

Hand-dyed silk Chenille is couched to outline the flowers of a motif.

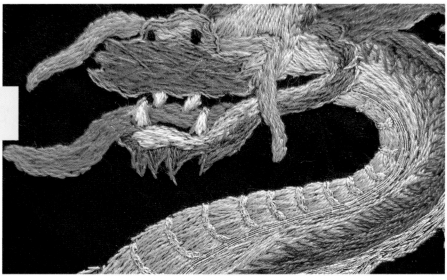

Gold metallic threads are used to highlight the dragon's body.

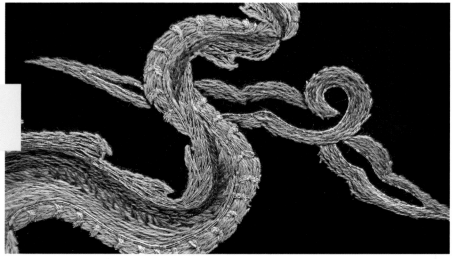

Japan thread is couched along the inner edge of the clouds to give them a silver lining.

Cross-stitch

Cross-stitch can be worked on evenweave fabric and then used for a quilt patch, *or* on a patched quilt top using waste canvas.

The fine art of cross-stitch comes alive when it is worked on linen fabric. Linen is available in a range of colors and weaves, and makes an ideal fabric to add to a crazy quilt. Work the embroidery before patching the quilt.

Materials

Waste canvas and
   background fabric, or linen
   evenweave fabric
Embroidery floss
Sharp or blunt needle

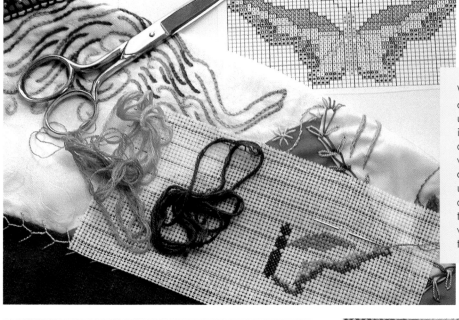

Working cross-stitch on fabrics that are not evenweaves requires the use of waste canvas. This canvas is basted onto the fabric, the design is embroidered, then the waste canvas is removed a thread at a time. A blunt needle can be used if the fabric allows, but in any case do not allow the needle to work into the threads of the waste canvas or it will be difficult to remove.

Cross-stitches are worked over two threads (they can also be worked over one thread, but this makes a very fine stitch). Work an individual stitch as shown. Use one, two or more strands of floss as needed to cover the background without distorting the weave of the fabric.

Work a row of stitches by doing one half of the stitch for the entire row, then turn back and work the remaining half.

The naïve style horse was worked on linen using cross-stitch in three shades: two browns and black. Choose your own colors and shade the horse to your liking (it is not necessary to carefully follow the chart).

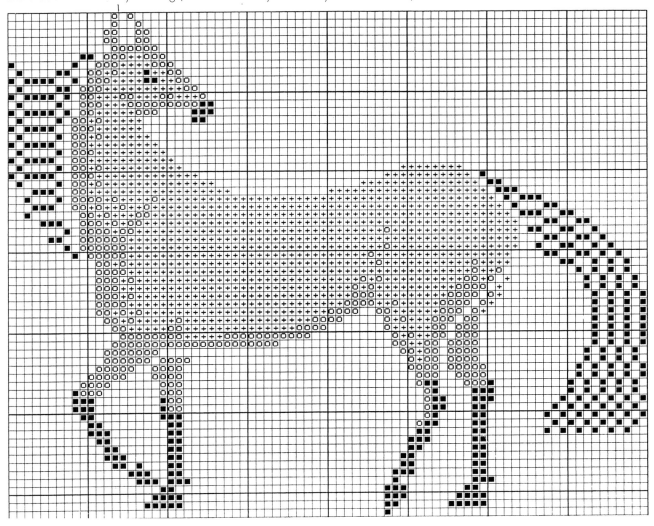

Needlepoint is similar to cross-stitch. There are a variety of stitches that can be used, and although the cross-stitch itself can be worked on needlepoint canvas, most needlepoint stitches resemble one-half of the cross-stitch. This intricate flower is a rose from my garden, carefully drawn and then translated into needlepoint. I tried it in two different color schemes, but do choose your own colors.

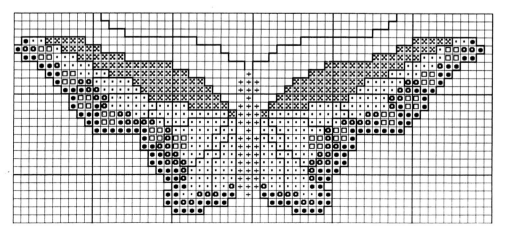

One of the butterflies from page 39 is here translated into graph form for cross-stitch.

Dimensional Clothing

Materials

Silk or other fabric scraps
Silk or cotton sewing thread, needle
Pins
Embroidery materials

An embroidered figure is "dressed" with scraps of fabrics, similar to appliqué, but the fabrics can be shaped as they are sewn. A similar technique was used by the Victorians to "dress" images of ladies on greeting cards. Begin by embroidering the outlines and details of the figure using the Tracing Paper Transfer Technique, page 141. To dress the figure, cut fabric pieces larger than the clothing will be. Tuck, pleat, and gather the fabric pieces to make them appear as actual clothing. Turn under the outer edges so there will be no raw edges. Pin as you shape. Using tiny stitches, stitch the clothing in place. Add any additional desired details.

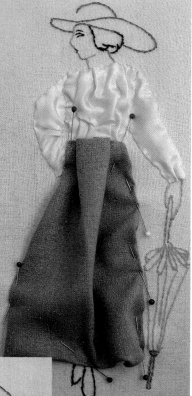

Above: This lady's silk blouse is sewn into place. Her skirt is pinned on top of the blouse.

Left: The skirt is sewn into place. Fill-in embroidery can be used to complete the design. Additional details may also be added such as tiny buttons on the blouse.

Drawing

Stylistic – when an object is shaped differently than it would be in reality. The classic heart-shape that we use for valentines is a stylistic rendering of a heart.

Realistic – an accurate rendering of an object.

Drawing is the single most valuable skill to learn if you wish to have unique images on your crazy quilt. I don't want to hear how you can't do it, or you can't do it in a straight line … *anyone can draw.* It is not a specialized skill, although it does take practice to draw really well. If you do it a little every day you can get good at it. A book that has helped many learn to draw beautifully is *Drawing on the Right Side of the Brain, A Course in Enhancing Creativity and Artistic Confidence,* by Betty Edwards.

Pencil and paper are all the tools you need. Here is my favorite thought regarding creativity:

Leave all thought matter behind and proceed with no caution.

Find your drawing style. Will you use a pen, pencil, or brush? Do you prefer bold, dashed lines, or delicately sketched lines? I, myself, lightly sketch outlines then go back and refine, adding details and shading. Sometimes this takes a bit of time. The earth goes round and the light changes on me. For me, drawing is meditative: My mind quiets and my hand draws. Try drawing meditatively, and also try drawing actively – putting all of yourself and your energy into it. Find what works for you. Drawing is like handwriting; what goes onto the paper is you and yours alone.

Drawing is a way to learn about things around you. Once you begin drawing, you may find that you see the world differently – more intently. You observe more carefully. Any learning is a good thing – it opens your mind to *more* learning!

Drawing puts objects into relationship with each other. Teach yourself to see those relationships as you draw.

You can draw by doing the outlines of things exclusively, or by using shading only. The two can also be combined. Perceive the true shapes of objects by drawing their outlines. Find the bulk or depth of things by learning to shade.

Drawn designs can be either stylized or realistic. True drawing attempts to accurately render an object, but designs can also be worked imaginatively. Take a look through the motifs in this book; you can determine which of them are realistic, and which are not. Drawings can be stylized by reshaping the realistic version, or by simply drawing from an idea that is in your mind.

You will need tracing paper and tape.

Some forms in nature, such as clouds and water, invite numerous linear interpretations. Try drawing a simple cloud form then proceed to invent others. Do the same with water. Do these freehand; tracing should not be necessary. See the cloud motifs on page 42, and the water motifs on page 134 for examples. See also Landscapes and Scenery on pages 87 to 89 for examples of drawing landforms and using photographs.

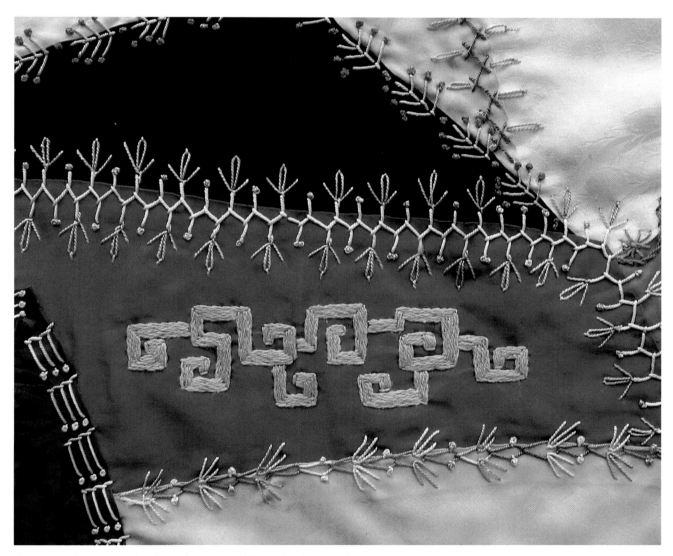

Geometric designs can be derived easily, and formed to fit a patch.

Building a Motif

Sometimes motifs can be combined to make a larger whole. Here, a small motif was redrawn three times then arranged in a coherent way. Also experiment with combining motifs to form rows, wreaths and other other formations, whatever you need to fit onto the patches of your quilt. Trace as many copies of the design as you will need, arrange them and tape them together. Retrace the final design to use it as a tracing paper transfer.

Fabric Flowers

Fabric flowers are best worked **after** the quilt top is patched.

Materials

Ribbons or scraps of silk
 fabric
100 percent cotton or silk
 sewing thread
Hand sewing needle, pins

Small pieces of silk fabrics and ribbons can be gathered into flower shapes and stitched down. Baste a line of running stitches and gather. Stitch the flowers onto the background fabric, and add a flower center or leaves. Flowers can be shaped as they are stitched. This white flower is being made of bias-cut silk ribbon.

Motifs for Fabric Flowers

Fans for Patching

Materials

Silk fabrics, small pieces
Fabric scissors, pins
Hand sewing needle, basting
  thread
Tracing paper, pencil, scissors

Read through the instructions before beginning any of the following pieced fan patterns. Most are patched directly onto the quilt's foundation, just as if they were fancy patches.

Fabrics other than silk may be used for most of the fans, although the fans shown were all made of silks. As with appliqué, fabrics should hold a crease and be disinclined to ravel. Use the tracing paper to trace the needed pattern pieces, and cut them out.

Plain Fan

Cut out the fan pieces from silk or other fabrics. Sew the blades together, either by machine or by hand. Press the seam allowances open or to one side. Place the sewn blades onto the quilt top, then add the fan's center, pressing under the rounded edge and slipstitching or basting in place.

Finish the outer edges of the fan by pressing under, or place surrounding patches onto these edges.

Work embroidery along the seams of the blades and the center, and around the fan itself.

This fan is made as the quilt top is being patched. For a colorful fan, cut each of the fan pieces of a different color of fabric.

Scalloped Fan

Make this fan the same as the Pieced Fan, except take care to form the scalloped edges of the blades. Press the scalloped edges under before assembling the blades.

Scalloped Fan with Heart Center

To make a similar fan, use the fan blade pattern for the Scalloped Fan, but cut each blade slightly shorter toward the outer edges of the fan. Observe the photo to see how this is done, and for the shaping done to the outer ends of the shorter blades. Ten blades are used, making the fan wider than the Scalloped Fan. For the fan center, cut out a heart shape, adding seam allowances. Press the edges under and appliqué onto the blades. Add embroidery as shown in the photo.

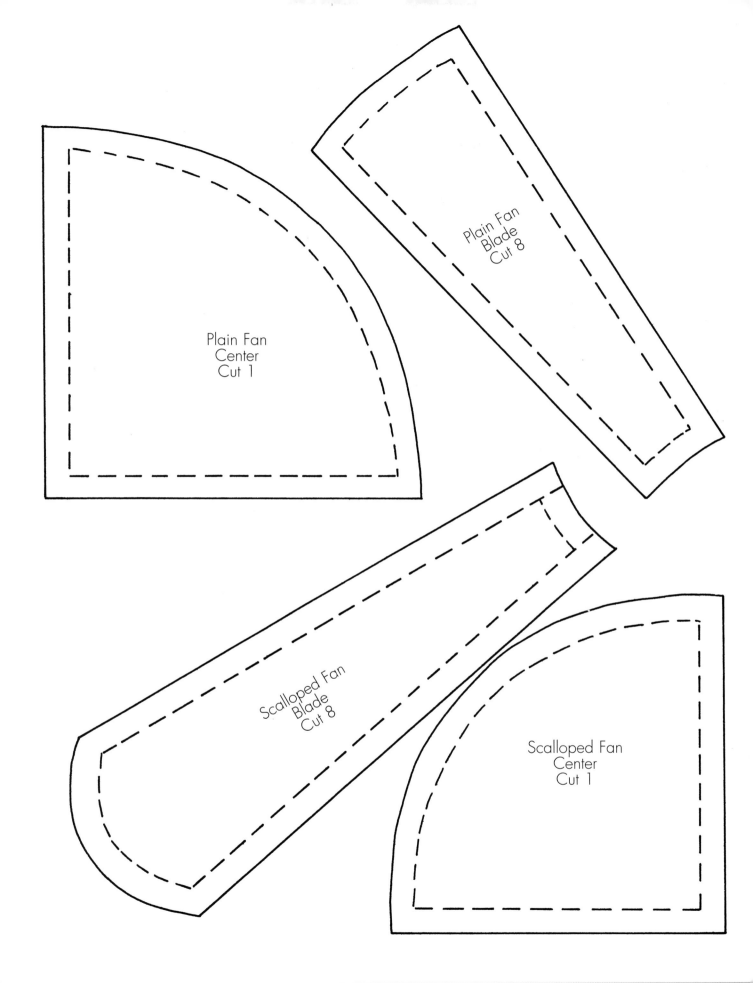

Plain Fan
Blade
Cut 8

Plain Fan
Center
Cut 1

Scalloped Fan
Blade
Cut 8

Scalloped Fan
Center
Cut 1

Appliqué and Silk Ribbon Fan

All the blades are 7mm silk ribbon. Place the ribbons, and add border and center.

You will need one yard of 7mm silk ribbon, all one color, or about 9 pieces each 4" long in the colors of your choice. This fan is added to a quilt patch, on an already-patched quilt top.

Cut the fan border and center pieces out of fabric, adding seam allowances all around each piece. Press under the allowances.

Lay 7mm silk ribbons in a fan shape, and add the fan center and outer border to cover the ends of the silk ribbons. Arrange the ribbons to fit with the fabric pieces. First pin, and then baste all in place. Secure the pieces by working embroidery along the ribbons, and slipstitching the fabric pieces.

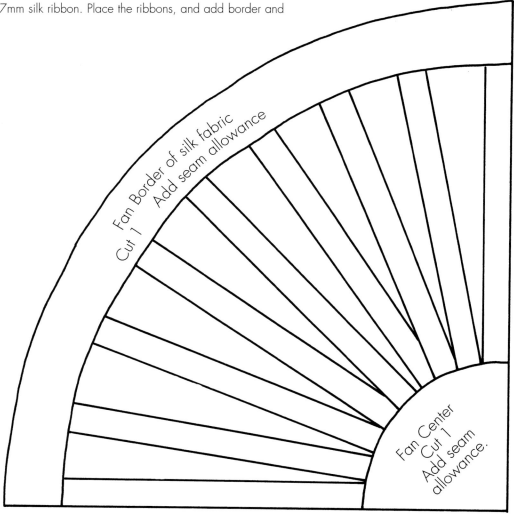

Fan Border of silk fabric
Cut 1
Add seam allowance

Fan Center
Cut 1
Add seam allowance.

Round Silk Fan

This fan is intricate, best reserved for the experienced needleworker. Silk is the fabric of choice because it is light enough to maneuver easily. Make it directly on a quilt foundation, adding surrounding patches after the fan blades are assembled. The blades of the fan are strips of fabric, laid consecutively from one side of the fan to the other. Make the blades in two colors as shown here, or in the colors of your choice.

First cut out the handle and center from the silk fabric of your choice. Press seam allowances under. Then cut narrow strips of fabric for the blades, adding about 1/2" to the width of each for seam allowance. Press under one long edge of each 1/4".

Draw the fan shape onto the foundation. Begin at one side and lay the strips, overlapping them. Observe the photo for approximate placements of the strips. You may choose to use fewer of them, as that will make the project easier. Pin and baste as needed, and trim the strips to fit within the drawn fan shape.

Add patches to the quilt top surrounding the fan, fitting them directly up to its raw edges.

Finish the outer edges of the blades by adding a bias-cut strip of fabric with its edges pressed under, or a ribbon, slipstitching it in place.

Add the handle and fan center, slipstitching in place onto the patches that were added around the fan.

Add embroidery stitches to secure the fan blades in place.

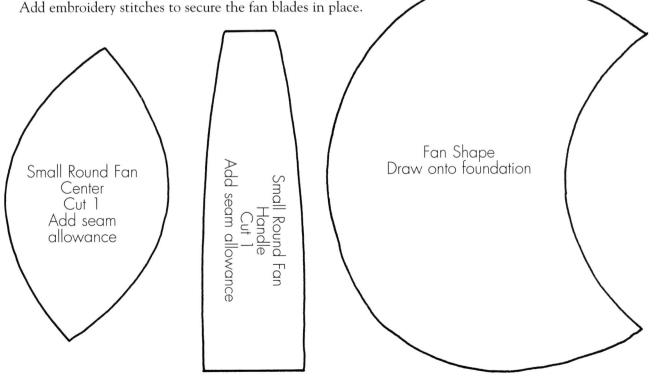

Small Round Fan
Center
Cut 1
Add seam
allowance

Small Round Fan
Handle
Cut 1
Add seam allowance

Fan Shape
Draw onto foundation

Large Silk Fan

This is made exactly the same as the Small Silk Fan but larger. Make the fan handle and center pieces the size of your choice, and form the blades to the width and length of your choice. A small silk ribbon embroidered motif was worked onto the fan center shown here.

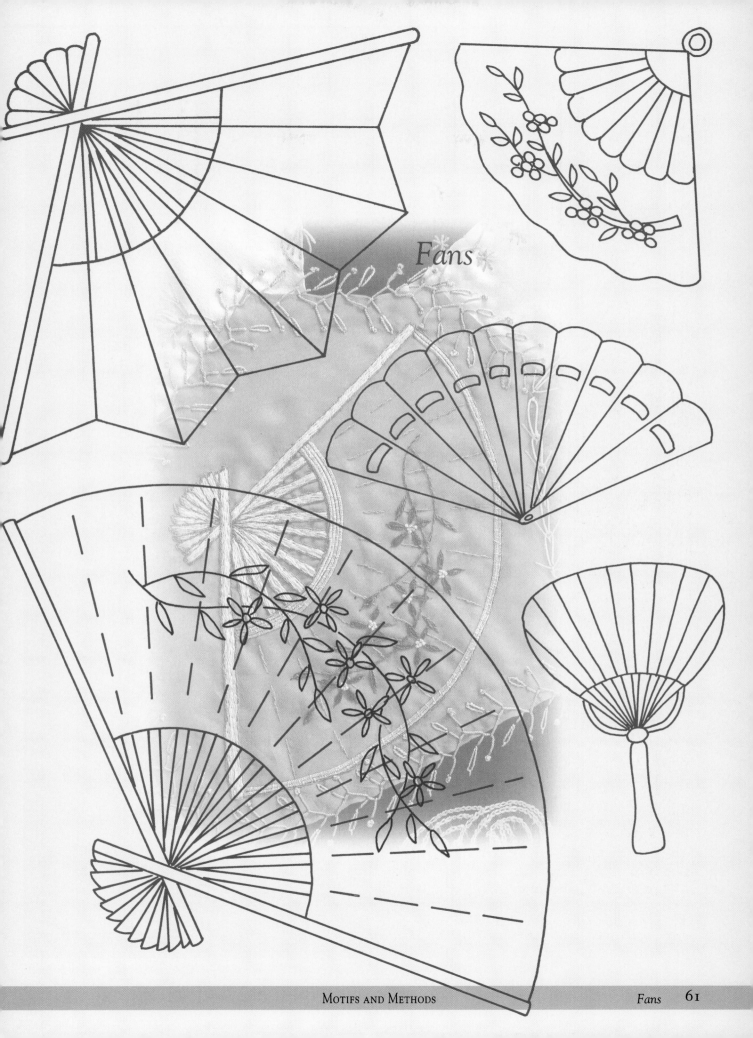

Fans

Feathers

Fern = Fascination

Fill-in Embroidery

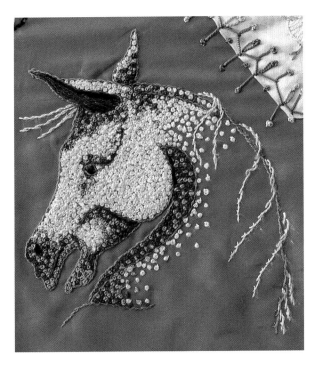

Fill in embroidery can be worked **before** or **after** the quilt top is patched. Doing fill-in **after** gives the foundation a place to park the beginnings and endings of threads.

Although any stitch that fills an area can be used to fill in an embroidery, the most commonly used are satin, and the long and short stitch. Outline stitch works well also, and French knots are useful for special effects. Try different stitches for filler work, and you will soon find your own favorites.

Techniques for fill-in embroidery include:

• Cut strands of thread a working length that you are comfortable with, anywhere from 18" to 36" long. For most threads, I reel off an "arm's length," keeping the lengths consistent. Consistency makes for faster stitching because you have a sense of how far to pull the thread when pulling through.

• For covering large areas, use a doubled thread.

• To fasten on a thread, do not knot the end; instead make several tiny stitches into the foundation fabric. Fasten off the same way. If there is no foundation, leave a loose end and work the first few stitches into it. End by running the thread through the backs of the last few stitches.

Top: Although time-consuming, French knots are an effective way to fill in motifs. Here, they assume the gray tones of a white horse.

Center: My favorite stitch for filler work is the outline stitch. I find it more "painterly," and it does not create the floats of the satin stitch. Floats can catch on things, making the finished quilt less practical for use.

Bottom: Note how the two gray shades of the bird's body are blended to make a smooth transition from one shade to the other. The bird is worked in outline stitch, using a single strand of Silk Mori.

The motif is outlined in backstitch in preparation for satin stitching. The satin stitches can be worked over the backstitching, concealing it. If the filler will be worked in outline stitch, then use the same stitch for the outline.

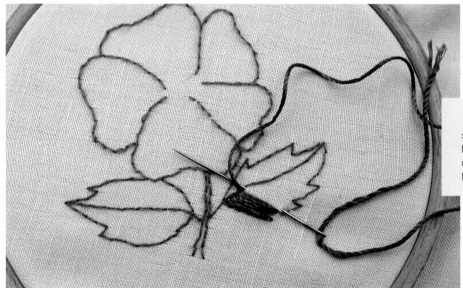

Satin stitch is worked by taking a stitch over the entire distance. Use this stitch for short distances only to avoid having long floats of threads.

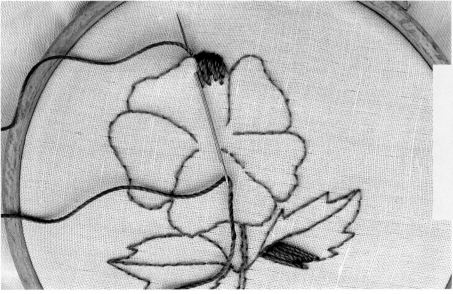

Long and short stitch is a variation of satin stitch, in which a short stitch is placed next to a long one. Use it for larger areas in order to make the stitches blend visually. Ideal for shading, each consecutive row of stitching can be worked in a darker or lighter shade of the color used.

Fish

Flowers

Although the flowers on the following pages can be traced and embroidered as they are, you can also use them to "build" your own bouquets. Begin with a flower and its stem, add another, and another. Draw the flowers free-hand, or trace them from the following pages. Fill in with smaller flowers around the edges, or use ferns. Make these in shapes that will fit your patches (trace the patch shape, then draw the flowers onto the tracing).

Other ways with florals include arranging them into swag or garland forms. Appliqué or embroider objects such as baskets, teacups, and other objects, then fill them with embroidered flowers.

Combine techniques to create larger bouquets: Begin with a folded flower or two, add an embroidered flower, then some silk ribbon flowers. You can begin with a basket or cornucopia and fill it with a lavish floral.

Gardening catalogs are an excellent source of flower pictures. Try drawing the flowers realistically, or stylize them.

Fuchsia = Taste

Trumpet Flower = Fame

Arum = Ardor

Marigold = Grief

Larkspur = Lightness

Dwarf Sunflower = Adoration

Columbine = Folly

Aster = Variety

Amaryllis = Pride. Splendid Beauty

Achillea = War

Daffodil = Regard

Mint = Virtue

Scarlet Poppy =
Fantastic Extravagance

Yellow Carnation = Disdain

Carnation = Alas! for my poor heart

Daylily = Coquetry

Coreopsis = Always Cheerful

Clematis = Mental Beauty

Buttercup = Ingratitude

Bell Flower = Gratitude

Goldenrod = Precaution

Candytuft = Indifference

Love Lies Bleeding = Hopeless, not heartless

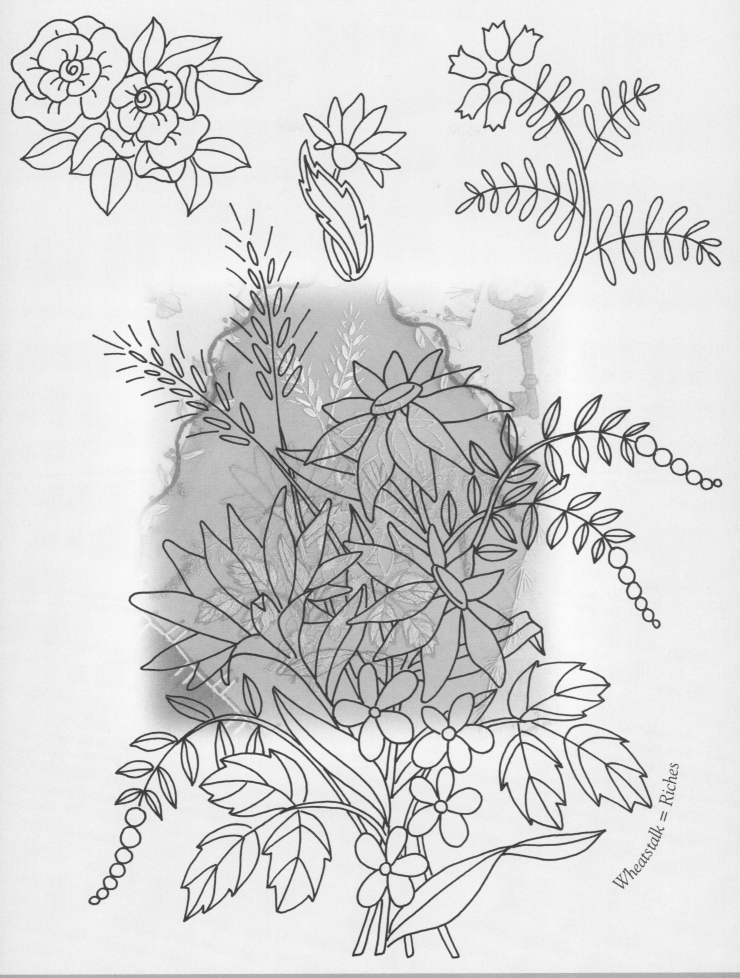

Wheatstalk = Riches

Hydrangea = A boaster
Heartlessness

Daisy = Innocence

Day Lily = Coquetry

Morning Glory = Affectation

Lilac = First emotions of love

Dahlia = Instability

Iris = Message

Flowers, Pansies

Pansy = Thoughts

Rose = Love

Maiden's Blush Rose =
If you love me,
you will find it out

Flowers, Roses

Yellow Rose = Decrease of Love. Jealousy

White Rose =
I am worthy
of you

Red Rosebud = Pure and Lovely

Single Rose = Simplicity

Moss Rosebud = Confession of Love

Deep Red Rose =
Bashful Shame

Cabbage Rose =
Ambassador of Love

Dog Rose =
Pleasure and Pain

Frames

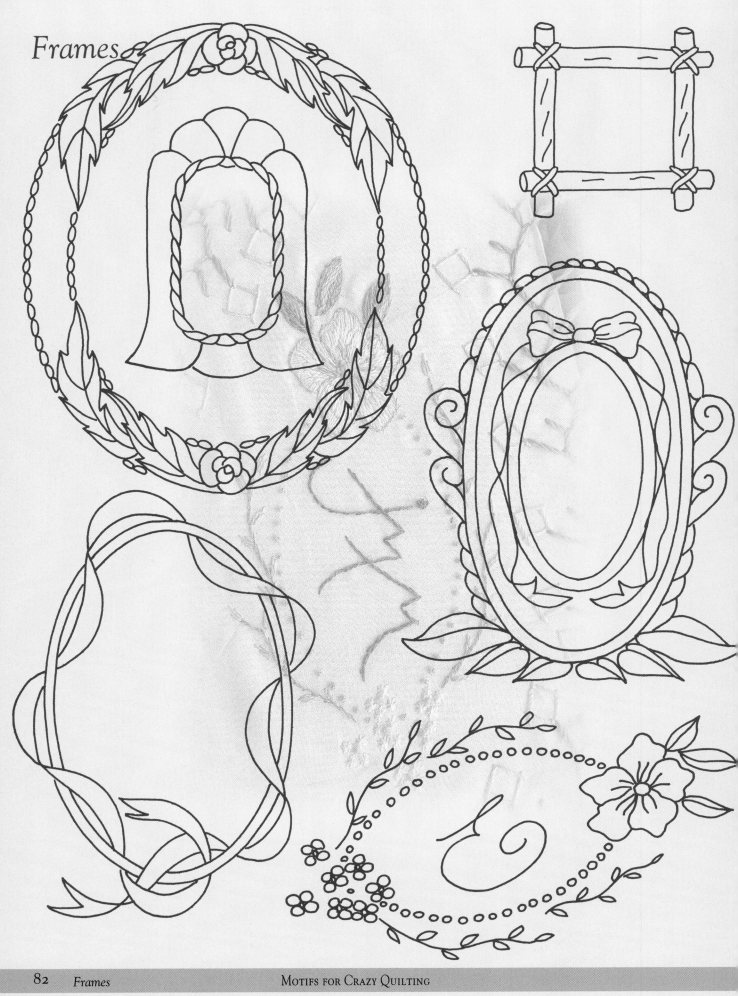

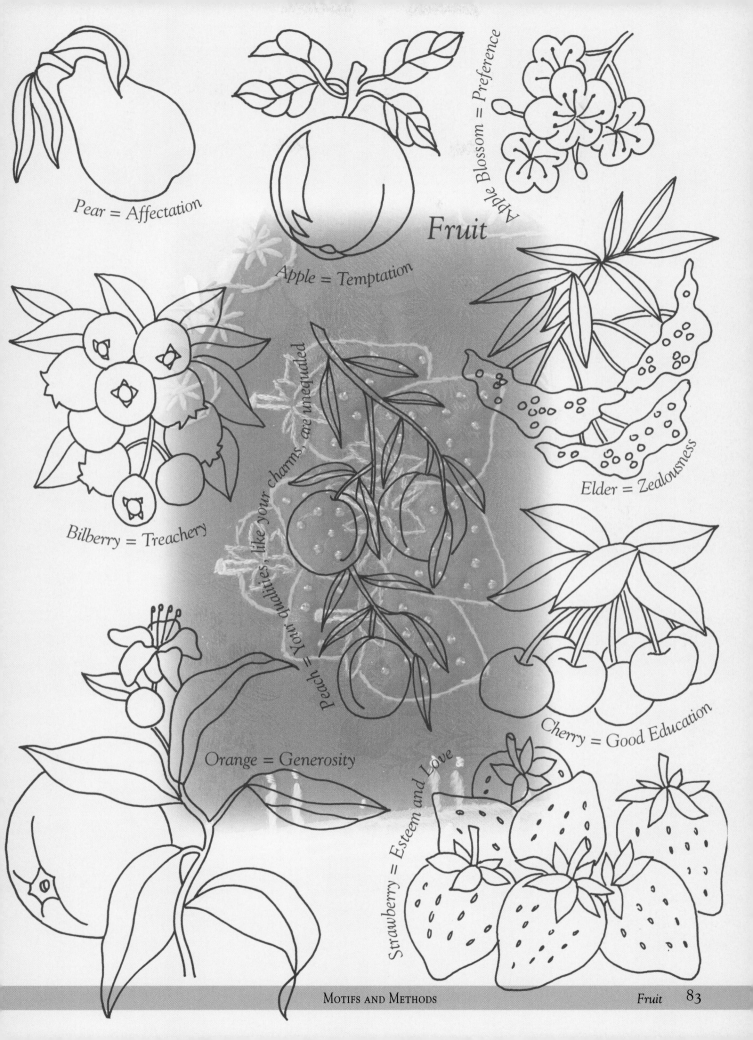

Pear = Affection

Apple = Temptation

Apple Blossom = Preference

Fruit

Elder = Zealousness

Bilberry = Treachery

Peach = Your qualities, like your charms, are unequaled

Cherry = Good Education

Orange = Generosity

Strawberry = Esteem and Love

Hearts

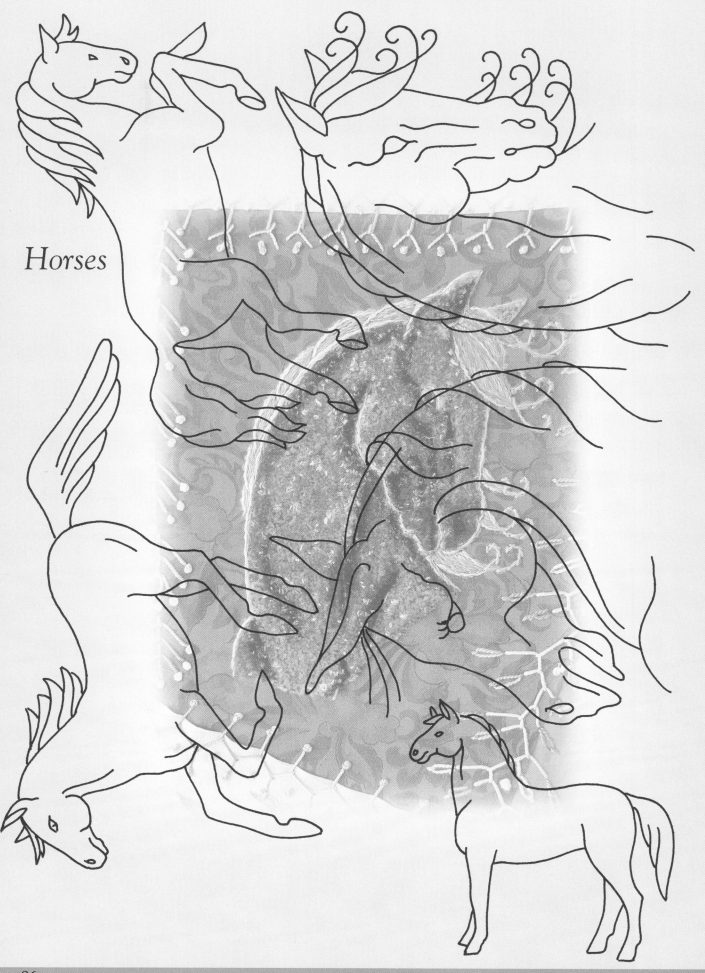

Horses

Landscapes and Scenery

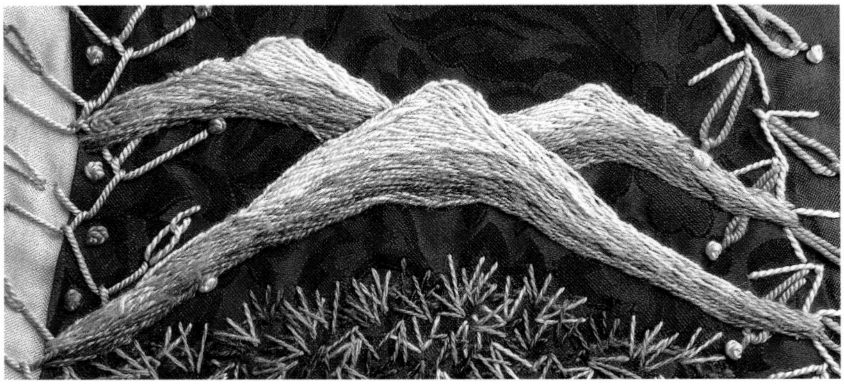

Mountains embroidered in Waterlilies.

To draw a landscape, find its basic form and draw its lines as shown here. Add details such as houses, trees, shrubbery, and clouds.

Your own photographs can be used as design ideas for landscape embroideries. Look for the most basic shapes, draw them, then embroider, fill in details as desired. Refer to the original photograph for colors, textures, and other details. These photos were taken by Rod Byam in Maine and New Hampshire.

Landscapes

MOTIFS FOR CRAZY QUILTING

Leaves

Mythical
Beings

Oriental Motifs

Grass = Submission. Utility

Peach Blossom = I am your captive

Lotus Leaf = Recantation

Peony = Shame: Bashfulness

Iris = Message

Outline Work

Outline work can be done **before** or **after** the quilt top is patched, although working it afterwards provides a place to anchor the threads.

Instructions for Outline Stitch

Use a fine embroidery needle with one strand of silk floss to obtain the finest outlining. Pair this with very fine stitches in the more detailed areas, and slightly longer stitches for the straighter or longer lines of the design.

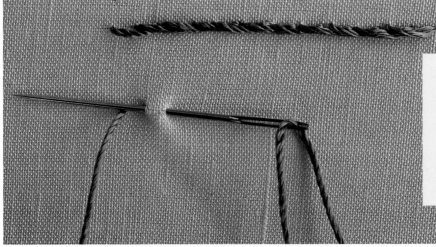

To make the outline stitch, bring the needle up through the fabric, and take the first stitch having the needle face where the thread comes through. Take the second and following stitches having the needle face the previous stitch. The stitch can be done with or without overlapping each consecutive stitch. Overlapping makes a thicker line.

Motifs worked entirely in outline stitch are charming additions to a crazy quilt.

Punch Needle

Set of punch needles in
sizes to accommodate
the threads you wish
to use
Punch needle threader
Embroidery hoop
Embroidery threads to fit
the needles

Punch needle requires two layers of fabrics, and so is worked **after** the quilt top is patched.

Punch needle is one of many ways to fill in a motif. It is used to create a pile of looped or cut fibers, is best suited for solid areas, and lends itself to shading. You will need a punch needle, a specially made needle for the purpose. They are available in a variety of sizes, and it is best to have several sizes on hand so that you can use different threads and fibers.

Punch needle is best worked through two layers – the crazy patch with its foundation underneath is ideal. It usually takes a few tries to learn, but don't give up – it is simple and quick once you get the hang of it. Thread the needle according to the instructions that came with it. The thread comes down through the shaft, then through the eye of the needle.

The needle has a flat side, and an open side where you can see the thread coming through. While punching, keep the open side facing upwards. Keep the tip of the needle in contact with the fabric between stitches. Develop a punch-slide, punch-slide rhythm as you punch. Always be sure the thread is unhindered so it can slide smoothly through the needle.

To fill a motif with needle punch, first outline the motif using outline stitch on the right side of the crazy quilt. This creates a backstitched outline on the reverse side.

Set the work snugly into an embroidery hoop with the wrong side facing up. Work from one side to the other of the design. Areas can be punched over again if the loops are not dense enough. When finished, the loops can be sheared using a very sharp scissors, or left looped, depending on the desired look for the design.

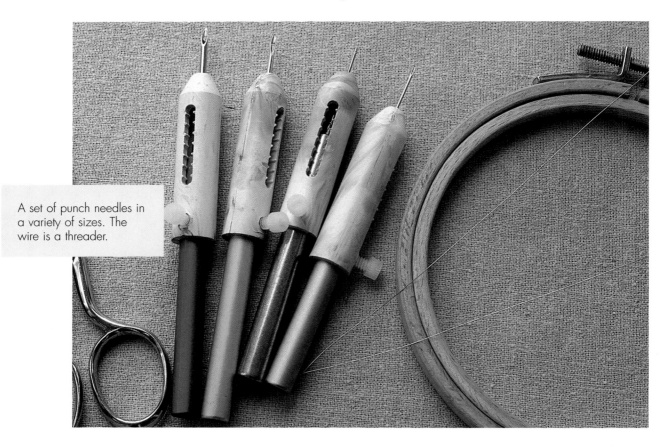

A set of punch needles in a variety of sizes. The wire is a threader.

Top: Use punch needle for parts of or whole designs. Here, a flower center is punched using one strand of Silk Mori.

Bottom: Punch needle makes attractive tree foliage. The tree is worked in one strand of Soie D'Alger.

Quilt Borders

Not to be overlooked, the border of a quilt provides additional area for decoration. Choose a design that is appropriate for the quilt, sizing it to be compatible with the width of the border. Designs can be done freehand, flowing continuously around the border, or by using a repeated motif.

Using the Tracing Paper Transfer Technique (see page 141), first make enough tracings. Place them around the border, spacing equally apart or as desired. Baste the tracings in place. If necessary, baste lengths of scrap fabric to each border, widening the border temporarily so an embroidery hoop can be used.

Top: A design such as this one can be worked freehand. First embroider a simple twining stem, then add leaves and flowers. Work the stem and leaves in pearl cotton, and the flowers in silk ribbon.

Bottom: Although not a motif as such, French knots en masse decorate the luminous rayon fabric of this border.

Top: A grouping of fabric flowers makes a motif that is repeated around the border of this quilt.

Bottom: The swag motif from page 104 was enlarged, and one swag was worked in the middle of each border. French knots in scalloped formation are worked continuously, connecting the swags.

Motifs for Quilt Borders

Rebus

A rebus is a sentence, phrase, or little poem put into pictures so it becomes a puzzle to the viewer. Make up a rebus of your own, and embroider it onto your quilt.

This rebus says (continued on the next page):
what shall i say?
what shall i do?
my lover has gone
and i am blue...

Sampler Motifs

Antiques, including samplers, can provide a wealth of embroidery design ideas. These samplers were designed and stitched by the author.

Sampler Motifs

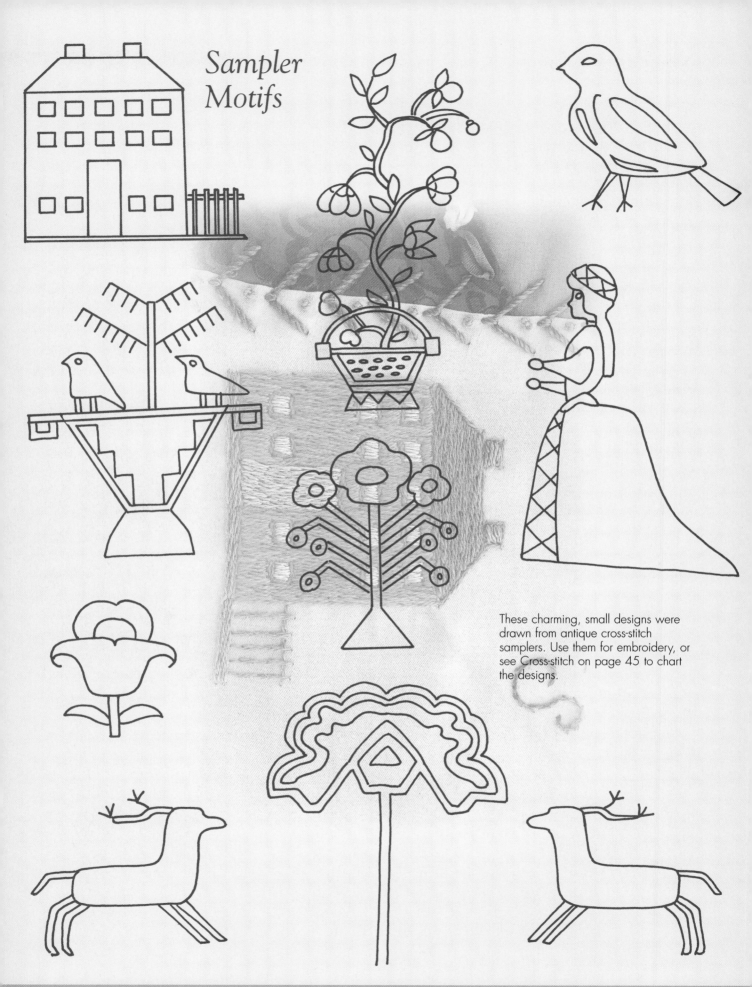

These charming, small designs were drawn from antique cross-stitch samplers. Use them for embroidery, or see Cross-stitch on page 45 to chart the designs.

Shadow Work

This method is worked **before** the quilt is patched.

Shadow work is the closed herringbone stitch worked on the reverse side of the fabric. The stitch is worked closely to fill in solid areas of a design and shows through the semi-sheer fabric as a shadowy effect. The stitch also forms a backstitch on the right side, neatly outlining the design. The reversed backstitch is used for any plain lines.

Shadow work must be done before the quilt top is patched since it is worked through only one layer. The finished shadow work embroidery may be laid over a color patch if it is desired that the color show through.

Semi-sheer fabric must be used to obtain the shadowy effect. Cotton organdy fabric is specified here because it has a stiffener in it that makes it easy to work on. 100 percent cotton batiste can also be used, although it is a soft fabric and not as easy to handle. Silk organza is a stiffened silk that may also be used.

The best designs consist of relatively narrow shapes that can be filled in with the herringbone stitch.

The method of transferring a design to the fabric is simple. Lay the fabric over the design, and lightly trace its lines. A hard lead pencil is preferable to keep the lines fine. The design is traced onto the reverse of the fabric, and will turn out backwards (keep this is mind if you are doing letters or words – the design must first be reversed).

Begin stitching at one end of a shape. To finish the thread ends, work over the tail of the beginning thread, and weave the end into the stitches already made.

Fill in each shape separately, finishing ends for each. Unless they are very close together, do not run threads from one shape to another – they will show through to the front.

Materials

100 percent cotton organdy fabric, white
Cotton embroidery floss, white or colors
Size 26 tapestry needle
Pencil

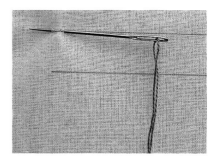

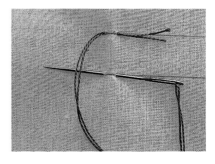

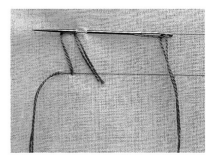

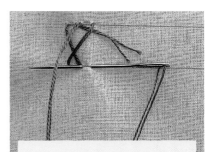

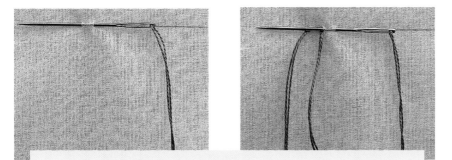

The Reverse Backstitch. With the needle facing to the left, make stitches immediately next to each other. The outline stitch will form on the surface, with a neat row of backstitches on the other side of the fabric.

The closed herringbone stitch. Stitch first at the top, then the bottom of an area to be filled in. Following stitches "borrow" the hole made by the previous stitch.

Work the stitch more closely in wider areas, and more widely in narrow ones.

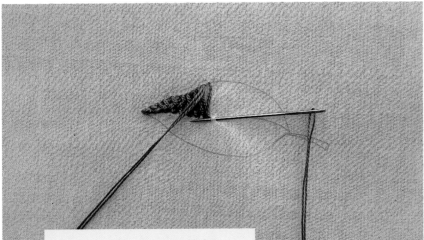

Top: To work a narrow leaf, first work reversed backstitch along its center, then fill the entire shape with closed herringbone stitch.

For a wide leaf, work one half in herringbone, then the remaining half in the same, but at the center work into the previous stitches instead of through the fabric to avoid a double line of stitching.

Right: Trace the design directly onto the fabric using a pencil.

Below: The back of the work, with embroidery finished.

Motifs for
Shadow
Work

Shells

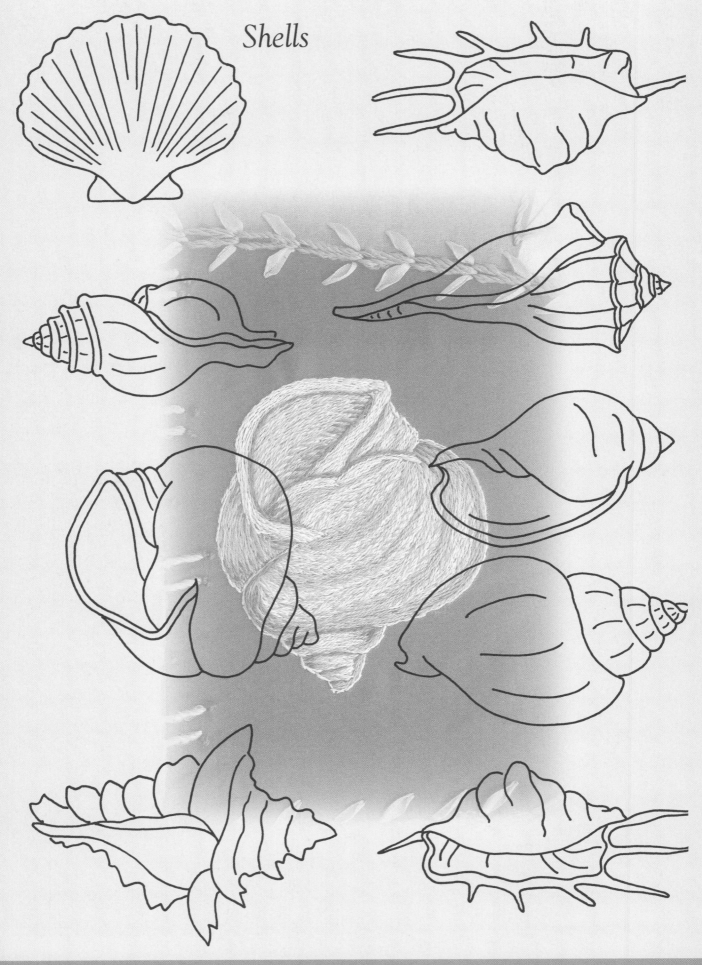

Silk Ribbon Florals

This method can be worked **before** or **after** the quilt top is patched, although doing so **after** provides an extra layer to work the ends into.

This is my most valued crazy quilt embellishment technique. It is easy to learn and to do, works up quickly, and the results are dimensional. Most often, stitches are made to imitate the shapes of flowers and leaves. Shading happens naturally by the effects of light and shadow on the ribbon.

Use an embroidery hoop if making individual embroideries on scraps of fabric. Use a quilter's lap hoop if working onto a patched quilt top.

Instructions for threading the needle, the ribbon stitch, and the loop stitch are given here. Other embroidery stitches are the same as for regular embroidery, and any embroidery stitches may be used especially lazy daisy, French knot, feather, cretan, and fly stitches. The stitches can be varied by forming them loosely (especially effective with French knots), or by twisting the ribbon. Make roses by working the outline stitch in a circle beginning at the center, or by working around a center of French knots. To vary the sizes of flowers and leaves, use ribbons of different widths.

Use a short length of ribbon (12" - 14") and a size 18 chenille needle to prevent excessive wear and tear on the ribbon. Press the ribbon on low heat if necessary.

Fasten on a ribbon by making a tiny stitch on the back of the work. Run the needle up through the fabric bringing the needle through the tail of the stitch. Fasten off by making two or three tiny stitches on the back.

Materials

Size 18 chenille needle
4mm silk ribbons, also 2mm and 7mm widths if desired
6" embroidery hoop or 14" quilter's lap hoop

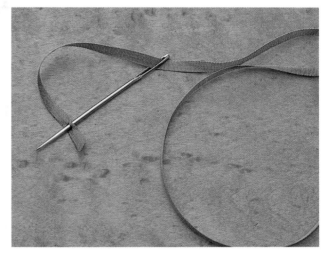

Top: Thread the needle by bringing the ribbon through the eye, then run the needle through the ribbon about 1/2" from the same end. Pull on the long end to settle the "knot" into the needle's eye.

Middle: The ribbon stitch is formed by laying the ribbon flat on the fabric and running the needle through to the back at the end of the stitch. Stop pulling on the ribbon as soon as the stitch forms as you like it.

Bottom: The loop stitch is made the same as the Ribbon stitch, but pull through closer to the beginning. Make the loop the size desired. The following stitch will hold it in place.

Establish the form of the design. Here, three roses and three ferns give the shape of the embroidery.

Add some leaves to the roses.

Embroider stems in thread, then add silk ribbon French knots. French knots are very useful for adding "filler" to a design that seems to need just a little bit more.

Floral Baskets in Silk Ribbon Embroidery

Here are some suggestions for working silk ribbon florals; try some of them, then devise some designs of your own. It is necessary to transfer only the outlines of the baskets. Outline each basket using outline stitch, and then fill them in by observing the diagrams and photos. You may also consider working your own floral ideas freehand.

Fill in the basket shape with a loosely made outline stitch, or use weaving. Add French knots, ribbon and lazy daisy stitches.

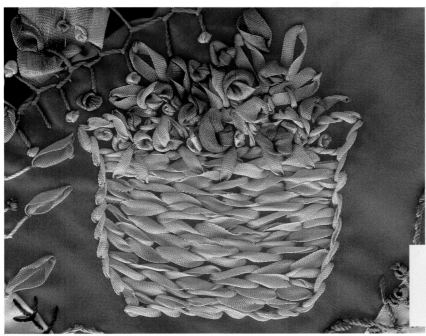

To form the basket, make long straight stitches, tacking them in place with French knots. Add some twisted straight stitch ferns, a couple of outline stitch roses, and some ribbon stitches and French knots.

Silk ribbon is perfect for small weavings. Place the vertical ribbons by making straight stitches. Weave through them horizontally, making each pass-through one long stitch. Fill the basket with ferns made of twisted straight stitch, adding flowers of loop, ribbon, and lazy daisy stitches.

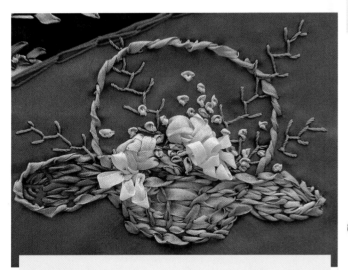

Use outline stitch to fill in this basket shape. Fill the basket with outline stitch roses, loop stitch flowers, and French knots.

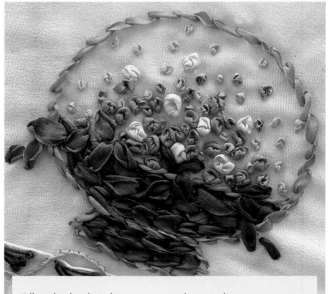

Fill in the basket shape using outline stitch or weaving. Fill it with French knots in various sizes, adding some ribbon stitch leaves.

This basket is filled in with outline stitch. Using 7mm silk ribbon, take a small stitch at the top of the handle, tie a knot, and arrange the bow as you like it. Pin the bow in place. With a 4mm silk ribbon, make tiny tacking stitches to hold the bow in place. Add flowers of ribbon stitches and French knots to the basket.

Spiders & Webs

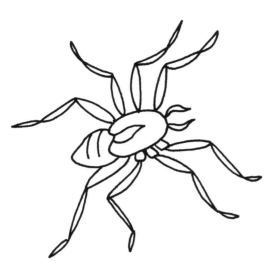

The finest webs are made by couching a fine thread. Use shimmery rayon or silk, or metallic thread. First, establish straight lines by couching single strands of thread. "Spin" the web lines by making stitches between the couched threads. Use the drawings for reference only, making webs to fit the sizes and shapes of your patches.

Spiders can be worked as detailed embroideries – or more simply by using beads or building up stitches for the body, then adding the legs.

Construct the web going from the edge of the patch to various places on a flower, as it would in nature.

Motifs for
Spiders & Webs

Symmetrical Florals

By doodling on a folded sheet of tracing paper, it is easy to create floriferous designs. Use the designs given here as examples, and create your own floral fantasy.

Begin with an urn or vase shape, making it in sections that can be filled in with embroidery. This type of design can be built upon as far as you like, making it a fun thing to work on. You can keep it fairly simple, or keep adding to make it as intricate as you like.

Add stem, leaf, and flower shapes, working upwards and outwards from the vase or urn. Stylize the shapes – they only need to hint at being florals. Combine shapes that can be filled in with linear elements, such as decorative curlicues, to be embroidered in any outlining stitch.

It may take a few tries to achieve a workable design, so don't be afraid to crumple and toss if your drawing isn't working! See "Drawing" on pages 50 to 51 for more information on creating your own lines.

When finished with the half drawing, trace the lines onto the other half of the paper.

Use the finished drawing as a Tracing Paper Transfer (see page 141). Embroider your design in any way you like.

Fold the paper in half lengthwise. Begin drawing one half of a design.

Flip the tracing paper, and trace the tracing onto the other half.

Tambour Work

With a hook, work tambour **before** the quilt top is patched. With an embroidery needle, work **before** or **after** the quilt top is patched.

Tambour work consists of a fine chain stitch that is used to create an outline, or to fill in a design. Although it was originally worked with a hook through one layer of fabric, it can also be done using an embroidery needle. Either way, the same result is achieved.

The stitch has a special, distinctive texture to it, and makes a solid, broad outline.

The examples shown here were worked in one strand of silk floss. Use the embroidery materials of your choice, and stitch as finely as possible. Note in the waterfall how the colors can be changed mid-row to achieve different effects.

The chain stitch.

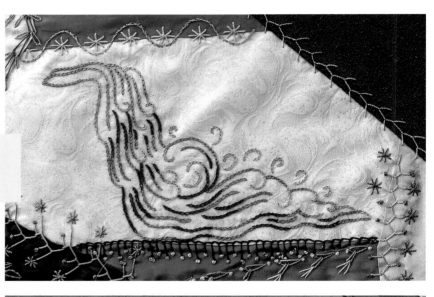

Tambour work is very effective for motifs worked entirely in outline. This waterfall is worked in Silk Mori.

Here, tambour work is being used as a filler stitch in Waterlilies.

Trapunto

Trapunto requires two layers of fabrics, so it is worked **after** the quilt top is patched.

Trapunto consists of adding stuffing to part or all of a design, padding it to give a dimensional effect. Crazy quilting offers the ideal support for this endeavor, in that the dual layer of the patch on the foundation provides a space that can be stuffed. Choose designs with outlined areas.

First, outline the design using any closely worked embroidery stitch such as outline or backstitch. Turn the work over to the back, and cut a small slit through the foundation fabric only. Be very careful not to cut through to the front.

Materials

Polyester or other stuffing fiber
Sharp-pointed embroidery
  scissors
Sewing thread and needle
Dull object for pushing the
  stuffing in

Using a small amount of stuffing (a tiny amount for a small area), push the stuffing through the cut opening and work it evenly into the area being stuffed. Use any tool that works. I use a metal nail file, or for a tiny area, the blunt end of a chenille needle. Then, sew the opening closed.

The dimensional petals require no additional embroidery.

Motifs for Trapunto

Trees

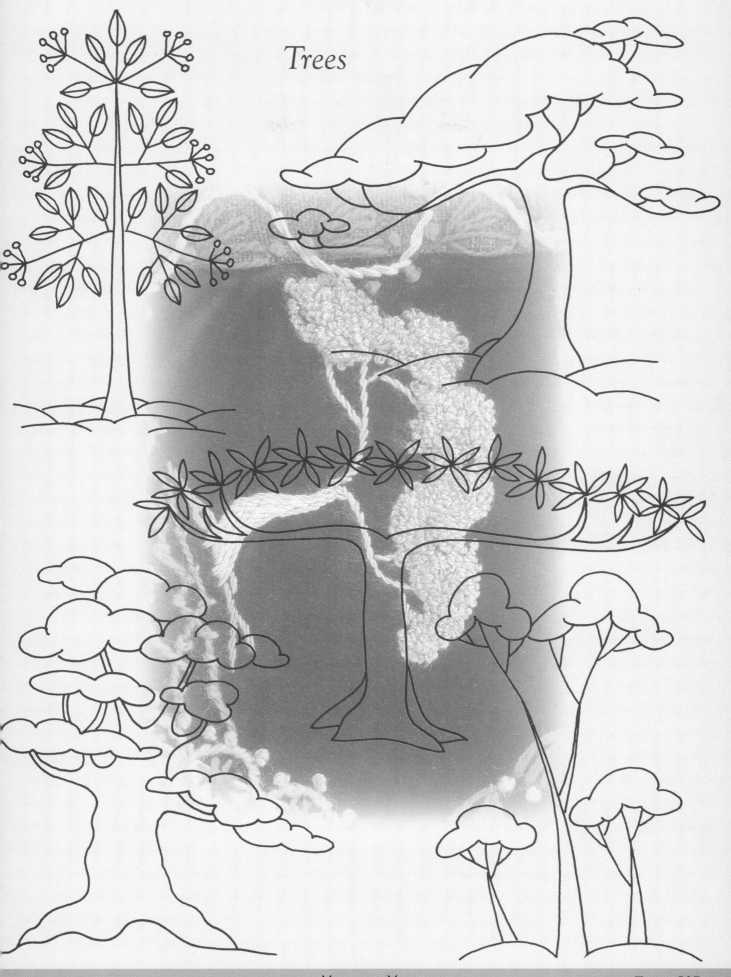

MOTIFS FOR CRAZY QUILTING

Vegies

Victorian Ladies

Motifs for Crazy Quilting

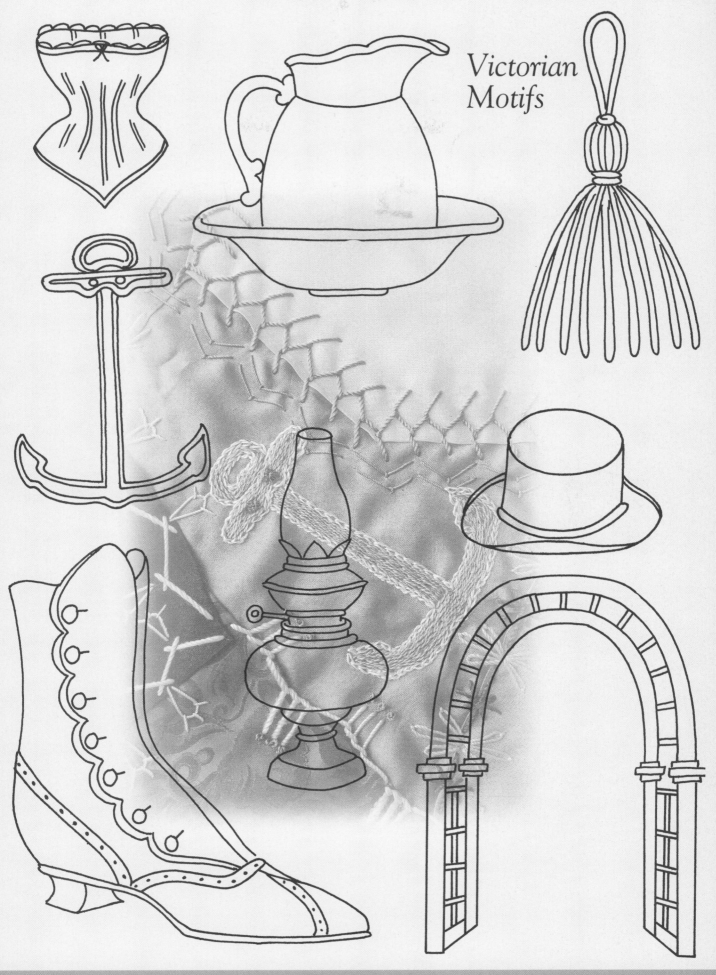

Victorian Motifs

Water

Embroidery needles to fit the
    threads
Embroidery floss or perle
    cotton, white or color of
    choice
Background fabric same color
    as floss
Embroidery hoop

Whitewark

Whitework is a technique that is subtle, yet beautifully decorative, consisting of working an embroidery design in white threads on white background fabric. Dimensional stitches such as padded satin, button-hole, and French knots are used, but almost any design can be used (see the accompanying motifs).

Experiment with different weights of threads to achieve different looks. Designs can be worked in heavier threads such as several strands of cotton embroidery floss or perle cotton for a "coarse" appearance, or in fine threads such as one strand of silk floss for a delicate, refined finish. Try whitework color on color instead of white on white, such as using a red thread on red fabric.

Padded satin stitch (see satin stitch on page 65) is the satin stitch worked over previously-made satin stitch, sometimes in three or more layers. The padding can also be a small piece of batting placed under the first layer of stitching. The early layers do not have to be neatly done; only the final layer should be worked carefully to give a neat appearance.

Detail of whitework, worked in ecru silk floss on off-white silk/linen fabric.

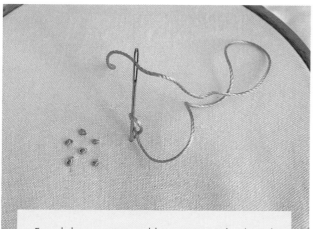

French knots are varied by wrapping the thread once, twice, or three or more times around the needle. Pull snug before pulling through. Learn the correct direction to wrap the thread, if wrapped the wrong way the knot will slip through the fabric and disappear.

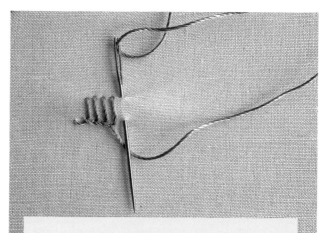

The buttonhole stitch is easy to do, requiring one pass of the needle. One edge of it creates an outline.

Motifs for Whitework

Raspberry = Remorse

Wool Embroidery

Materials

Chenille needles in sizes to fit the threads

Wool threads such as DMC Broder Medici, Paternayan Persian, and/or Caron's Impressions (a silk/wool blend)

Embroidery hoop if needed

Wool embroidery can be worked **before** or **after** the quilt top is patched, but is best done **after** to have a place for the ends of threads.

Wool embroidery consists of a variety of stitches that are often dimensional. Similar to silk ribbon embroidery, stitches are used to mimic the forms of flowers and leaves. Also like silk ribbon, this type of embroidery adapts well to freeform usage. Use it to build up floral bouquets, or to scatter flowers here and there on a patch.

Use a background fabric that can be embroidered easily. Wool and linen make excellent backgrounds, but other fabric types may also be used.

The needle should be a size to make a large enough hole in the fabric so the thread can pass through with minimal binding. If wool threads are allowed to bind they will fray and wear. Use single or double strands of wool, depending on the effect you wish to obtain.

Experiment with a variety of embroidery stitches to form floral and other motifs. Try some of the motifs shown in the photos, then do some freeform ones, combining floral forms into bouquets and sprays.

Try combining wool with silk ribbon or other types of embroidery for a wider range of textures and effects.

To form a rose, first make a center of French knots, then in a second color, work outline stitch around the knots until the rose is as large as you like it.

Bullion stitch makes beautiful roses and flower petals. To make the bullion stitch, take a stitch but do not pull through. Wrap the needle evenly, then hold the wraps in place while pulling the needle through. Go back down where the stitch began and give a little tug, if necessary, to even out the wraps.

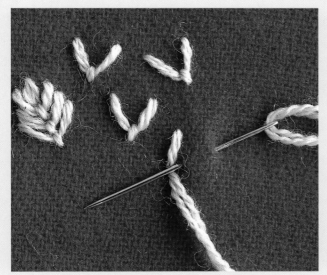

Make leaves of fly, lazy daisy, double lazy daisy, or any stitch that forms a leaf shape.

Detached buttonhole stitch is a matter of working buttonhole stitches onto a straight stitch without piercing the fabric. Use them for petals or leaves.

Sprigs of lavender are formed by first embroidering stems of outline stitch, then adding French knots.

Use a variety of stitches to form a bouquet, then add a bug!

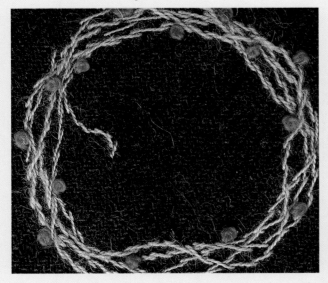

Form a wreath by working outline stitch around and around, then add a few French knots.

Wreaths

MOTIFS FOR CRAZY QUILTING

The Tracing Paper Transfer Technique

Materials

Artist's tracing paper
Hard lead pencil, scissors
Design to be transferred
Basting thread, needle
Quilter's lap hoop

This is the only method I use for transferring designs. It is simple, requires few materials, and leaves no marks on the fabric.

Trace the design onto the tracing paper. Use a hard lead pencil since softer leads can coat the threads.

Cut out the tracing, leaving about 1/2" excess paper all around. Baste the tracing to the quilt patch. I like to have the fabric or quilt top in a lap hoop until the design is entirely outlined in embroidery. The hoop provides the needed stability to keep the tracing paper from crumpling and tearing.

Embroider along the drawn lines.

After embroidering the outlines, carefully remove the paper by tearing it away, taking care to not disturb the stitches. In finely detailed designs, a tweezers may be needed to remove the extra bits of paper.

Note: Tissue wrapping paper may also be used. It is easier to remove afterwards, but the pencil lines will not show up as well – especially on dark fabrics – and it is less stable.

Steps in Making a Crazy Quilt

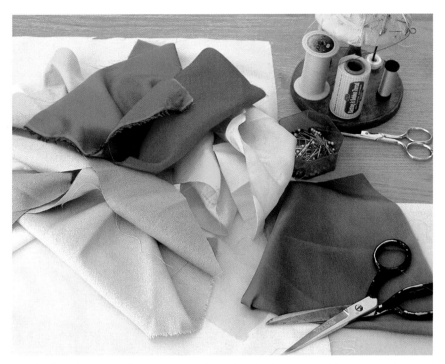

Lay the foundation out flat. An ironing board pushed up to a table supports the foundation and allows plenty of working area. Fabrics have been selected to make up a color scheme that includes bright colors and neutral tones. The necessary tools include iron, fabric shears, pins, needles, basting thread, and embroidery scissors.

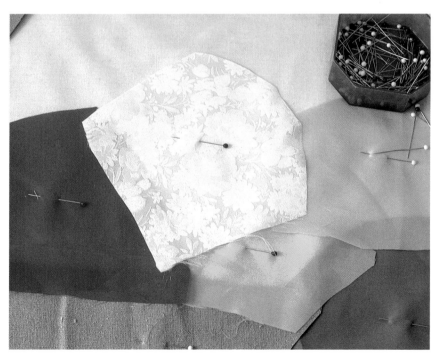

Begin anywhere on the foundation. Lay the patches so they over-and underlap by at least 1/2". Cut them into the shapes and sizes you prefer, allowing for the sizes of embroideries and embellishments you will be adding later. Pin each patch as it is placed.

Begin with a foundation fabric such as 100 percent cotton muslin, 100 percent cotton batiste, or silk organza, depending on the type of quilt or project. Muslin is the best choice for beginners because it provides a firm surface. Batiste and silk organza are for projects in which drape is desired such as shawls. Handle these carefully since they have a tendency to shift and bunch. Always prewash the foundation fabric.

Following are general instructions for finishing the quilt. For more details in finishing, consult any of my other three books on crazy quilting.

1. Work embroidery stitches along the seams of the patches, and embroideries within the patches.

2. Add a border if one is desired. Determine an appropriate width (one that looks good in relation to the quilt), and then cut the strips adding a seam allowance to each of the four edges. Make two that fit along the sides of the quilt. Sew them on. Then make two that fit along the top and bottom of the quilt, and sew them on. It is a good idea to line the border strips with the same fabric used for the foundation of the quilt. Work the embroidery design of your choice around the border (see Quilt Borders, page 102).

3. A batting is not needed in a crazy quilt, since the foundation fabric acts as one. However, if you wish to make a loftier quilt, add the batting of your choice.

4. Make a backing for the quilt, assembling fabric as needed to make the same size as the quilt with its borders.

5. Assemble the layers, having the backing face down, then the batting if one is used, then the quilt top face up. Pin or baste to hold the layers in place.

6. Finish the outer edges of the quilt with self-made or purchased bias binding.

7. Tie the quilt making the ties on the back of it. To tie, thread a needle with several strands of embroidery floss, or use one strand of pearl cotton. Make a tiny stitch, then cut the ends about 2" long. Tie the ends in a square knot.

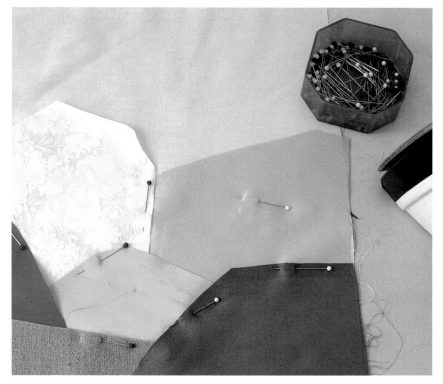

Carefully press under all of the overlapped edges. You may need to remove some of the patches to do this. Lay them back in place and pin. Check that all patches are over- or underlapped by at least 1/4" throughout. If not, adjust or add patches.

Begin basting when a large enough area of patching is completed. You can also patch the entire quilt top before beginning to baste if you prefer. Work on a surface that won't be damaged by scratches such as a cutting mat.

Other Books by this Author

The Magic of Crazy Quilting, A Complete Resource for Embellished Quilting. Iola, Wisconsin: Krause Publications, 1998.
Complete embroidery stitch instructions, 1,000 stitch variations, hand embellishments, patching/piecing methods, instructions for finishing a crazy quilt, color photos of contemporary and antique crazy quilts.

Crazy Quilts by Machine. Iola, Wisconsin: Krause Publications, 2000.
Designs for crazy quilts, four piecing/patching methods, techniques for machine embroidery and embellishments.

Crazy Quilted Heirlooms and Gifts. Iola, Wisconsin: Krause Publications, 2001.
Many projects to make, from home decor to gift items, and includes two methods of piecing/patching.

Ribbon Embroidery, 178 Iron-on Transfers. Mineola, NY: Dover Publications, Inc., 1997.
Instructions for silk-ribbon embroidery, and motifs suitable for crazy quilts and other uses.

Shadow Work Embroidery, With 108 Iron-on Transfer Patterns. Mineola, NY: Dover Publications, 1999.
Instructions for shadow work, motifs that can be used for shadow work and other types of embroidery, suitable for crazy quilts.

Design and Knit the Sweater of Your Dreams. Krause Publications, 2002

Index